Identifying and Correcting Reading Difficulties in Children

Identifying and Correcting Reading Difficulties in Children

Wilma H. Miller

The Center for Applied Research in Education, Inc.
New York

THE CENTER FOR APPLIED
RESEARCH IN EDUCATION, INC.
NEW YORK

Library of Congress
Catalog Card Number: 78-162014

PRINTED IN THE UNITED STATES OF AMERICA
C–3501–8

To D. M. S.

with sincere gratitude

About the Author

Wilma H. Miller, a former elementary teacher, now teaches at the college level. She completed her doctorate in reading at the University of Arizona under the direction of the late Dr. Ruth Strang, a nationally-known reading authority. Her doctoral dissertation on reading received a citation of merit from the International Reading Association in 1968. Dr. Miller is a frequent contributor to professional journals and the author of a new textbook for developmental reading, *The First R: Elementary Reading Today,* published by Holt, Rinehart & Winston, Inc. She is currently Professor of Education at Illinois State University, Normal, Illinois.

About This Book

Most elementary teachers would be very willing to help the moderately disabled readers in their classroom if they really understood the reading skills that a corrective program is based upon. Because of the financial help given to school districts by the federal government at the present time, a number of classroom teachers are becoming special reading teachers. These new reading teachers need books to which they can refer to help them understand the philosophy, the methods, and the materials that must be considered in any reading improvement program. The reader should understand that this book is not designed to take the place of graduate courses in reading but rather to supplement them with a practical book describing how to carry out a good program of reading improvement for most disabled readers.

This book was written for the inservice elementary classroom teacher who wants to correct the reading difficulties of the moderately disabled readers in her classroom effectively before these reading problems become so complex that they require special reading help in the clinic. If elementary teachers really knew how to correct these minor difficulties in the elementary classroom, many children would not have to receive special help in a reading clinic. This book also was designed for both novice and experienced special reading teachers in the elementary school or private reading clinic who want to add to their skill in conducting a remedial reading program. The book also may be helpful for the elementary-school reading consultant as she helps both classroom teachers and special reading teachers to better understand the methods and materials that can be used in a reading improvement program.

Five major divisions make up this book. First, the complex reading process is explained in a non-technical way since all reading teachers need to understand the various aspects of reading if they are to do a good job in conducting a reading improvement program.

The second division describes many of the causes of reading difficulties and illustrates how both standardized and informal tests can be used to diagnose specific reading difficulties. The third section of the book deals with the correction of reading difficulties and gives many practical suggestions on how to use children's interests and abilities in building the reading improvement program. This part of the book suggests many methods and materials for correcting specific word recognition and comprehension difficulties. This section also describes methods and materials for helping slow-learning children, reluctant readers, and culturally disadvantaged children to improve their reading ability. Of course, the special needs of disadvantaged children are very much in focus at the present time.

The fourth section of the book contains a brief but comprehensive survey of all the modern approaches to elementary reading instruction. Each teacher should thoroughly understand each of these methods so that she can use any of them in a reading improvement program if she needs to. The final division of the book concerns the role of parents both in preventing and in helping to correct their children's reading difficulties. This section is important because every elementary teacher often is asked by parents of preschool children how to prevent reading failure in school. Such information is especially important at a time when so-called panaceas such as "how to teach your baby to read" are publicized in popular magazines. Teachers often are asked by parents how they can help their child with his reading difficulties at home without harming the progress that is being made at school in the reading improvement program.

The reader will find the following to be the unique characteristics of this book which make it different from other books in this area:

1. The reading process is explained in a comprehensive and accurate way, but also in an easy to understand manner. The reader needs to understand the reading process so that she can determine in which facet of reading a disabled reader may be weak.

2. The causes of reading difficulties are explained in a non-technical, but in an accurate way. The book also presents the useful multiple causation theory of reading difficulty.

3. Criteria for determining if a child really is a disabled reader are presented. The reader then is helped to tell the difference between disabled readers and slow-learning children.

4. The reader is shown a practical way to construct, give, and score the individual reading inventory, a very useful diagnostic device for determining reading levels and specific reading difficulties.

5. The book clearly differentiates between corrective and remedial reading instruction, but illustrates how they are similar. The reader also is shown how children's interests and active involvement can help them to achieve success in the reading improvement program.

6. The book contains separate chapters for the correction of word recognition and comprehension difficulties. Many practical suggestions and a comprehensive list of materials are presented on how to teach all of the word recognition and comprehension skills.

7. The reader is shown how to differentiate between slow-learning children, disabled readers, and reluctant readers. The reader also is given many practical suggestions in both methods and materials for teaching reading to slow-learning children, reluctant readers, and culturally disadvantaged children.

8. The book describes all of the modern approaches to elementary reading instruction in a useful manner. The reader is helped to decide the values and limitations of each of these approaches and how to use each of them alone or in combination in any reading improvement program.

9. The educator will be able to involve parents in the prevention and correction of reading difficulties as much as their background of experience will allow. Correction of reading difficulties often cannot be completely successful if the cooperation of parents is not enlisted in some way.

It is hoped that the reader will find this book to be easy to understand and very useful. Certainly it is the right of every elementary-school child to read as well as his capabilities permit. This book can help the reader accomplish this purpose for many of the children that she is teaching.

Wilma H. Miller

Table of Contents

Identifying and Correcting Reading Difficulties in Children

1

The Reading Process

The act of reading is a very complex process with a number of interrelated parts. Reading consists of eye movements, word recognition, and the association of words with the experiences that they represent. Reading also consists of understanding what is read, evaluating what is read, and using the knowledge and attitudes gained from reading in the reader's own life in some way.

This chapter describes these parts of the reading process in detail and shows how a reader can have difficulty with any one of these aspects. The chapter also illustrates how each phase of reading is built upon the preceding ones. It further discusses how the teacher's view of the reading process can make a difference in which aspects of reading are emphasized for any child.

The Eye Movements in Reading

The first part of the reading process deals with the way a reader's eyes move across a line of printed material. Eye movements have been studied quite extensively for most of this century. At the present time, Miles Tinker of the University of Minnesota probably has spent more time studying eye movements than has any other reading specialist. Today eye movements are photographed by the Reading Eye Camera (Figure 1-1) which has

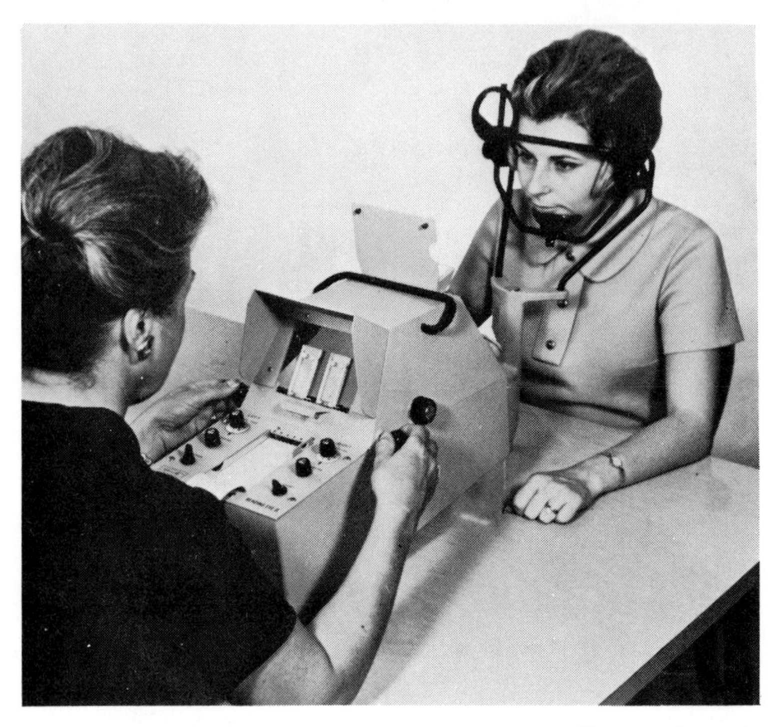

—Photograph, courtesy of
Educational Development Laboratories, Inc.

FIGURE 1-1

been developed by the Educational Development Laboratories.[1] This camera photographs eye movements while the reader is reading a printed page, and the movements look as shown in Figure 1-2.

Eye movement photography has found that the eye movements of readers are about the same in all alphabetic languages. The eye movements of most children do not change very much after they have reached the fourth grade reading level, but remain about the same for the rest of their lives.

The teacher can observe eye movements in an informal way through the use of the "peep-hole" method which Tinker described in the following way:

[1] "The Reading Eye," Educational Development Laboratories Incorporated, Huntington, New York.

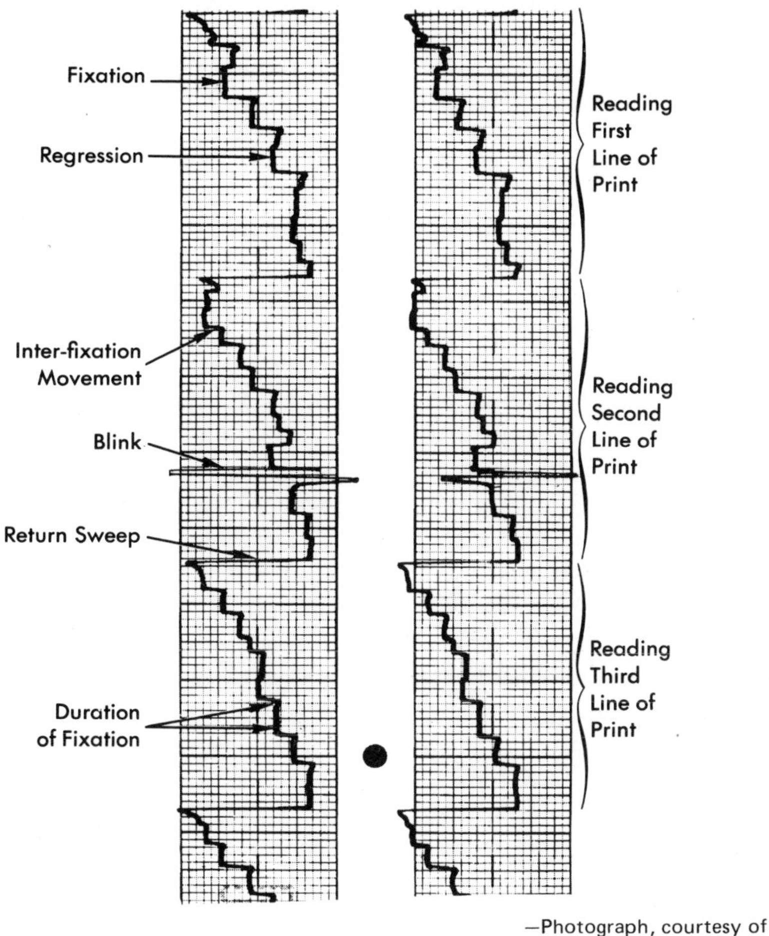

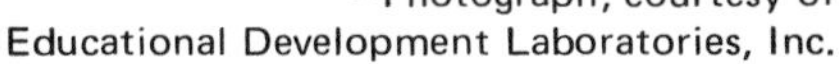
—Photograph, courtesy of
Educational Development Laboratories, Inc.

FIGURE 1-2

On a nine by twelve (9 x 12) cardboard attach two paragraphs of six to ten lines of reading material of appropriate difficulty, one paragraph just above the center of the card and the other just below the center. In the middle of the cardboard cut a small hole, one-fourth to three-eighths inches in diameter. Hold the cardboard at the proper reading distance directly in front of a pupil and place your eye immediately behind the opening. You now have the most advantageous viewpoint from which to see the successive movements and fixation pauses of one of the pupil's eyes as he reads the material on the cardboard. The movements are seen most easily

> when you fixate your attention upon the dividing line between the colored zone and the white of the pupil's eyes. This technique usually helps the teacher to determine whether a pupil's eye movements are very good or very poor in comparison with the rest of the children in the class.[2]

While a person is reading, his eyes move across the line of printed material in quick, jerking movements which are called *saccadic movements.* A reader does not recognize words when his eyes are moving, but instead he recognizes them when his eyes are pausing in *fixations.* A reader's eyes move only about six percent of the time while he is reading and they pause the rest of the time. While he is reading, a person recognizes most of the words by only noticing either the first few letters or the total shape. He stops to carefully analyze only those words that he has not had considerable experience with in his reading.

Of course, in the English language the eyes travel across a line of printed material from left to right in what is called *left-to-right progression,* and if a reader sees a word that he does not immediately recognize, his eyes move back to the unknown word in a *regression.* If there are too many new words in a passage, a reader makes so many regressions that often he completely loses track of what he is reading. The vocabulary control found in basal readers is mainly designed to eliminate regressions. This is also why it is important for a teacher to give a disabled reader material that is easy for him to read so he will not make too many regressions to have good comprehension.

A reader's eyes always are moving in advance of the point at which he is understanding what is being read, and this advance movement of the eyes is called the *span of recognition.* The teacher can determine a student's span of recognition by letting him read orally and then covering the end of the line with a card and seeing how long he can read orally with the line covered. There are two ways to increase a reader's rate of reading—either the length of the fixation pause must be shortened or the span of recognition must be made longer.

Most reading specialists believe that a classroom teacher need not be very concerned with the role of eye movements in reading.

---

[2]Miles A. Tinker, "Eye Movements in Reading," Reprinted from the May, 1959, Issue of *Education,* p.576, by permission of the Bobbs-Merrill Company, Incorporated, Indianapolis, Indiana.

Instead of working directly to improve eye movements, a better way to increase a reader's efficiency in eye movements is to give him much easy and interesting material to read. As the child's reading improves, his eye movements will improve, and he probably will have fewer regressions and shorter fixation pauses. Presently eye movements in reading do not receive much research since the understanding of them probably already has contributed as much as possible to the understanding of the reading process.

Word Recognition

The recognition of words as wholes or parts of wholes usually is considered to be the next part of the reading process. Of course, word recognition depends first upon the way the eyes move while reading. Word recognition, sometimes called word perception, is composed of the techniques of word form clues, phonetic analysis, structural analysis, picture and context clues, and dictionary usage.

Word form clues are among the more useful recognition techniques and consist of recognizing a word by its total shape, form, or configuration. Word form clues are one of the first word recognition techniques that a child learns to use in first grade, and they are also very useful for an adult reader. When a person is an efficient reader, he usually only needs to see the first several letters of a word or its total shape before recognizing it. The upper half of a word is very useful in recognizing it and can be illustrated by covering the bottom half of a line of print with an index card as shown in Figure 1-3.

Configuration is the drawing of a line around a word to help the reader to notice the unique shape of the word. The following is an example of the use of configuration:

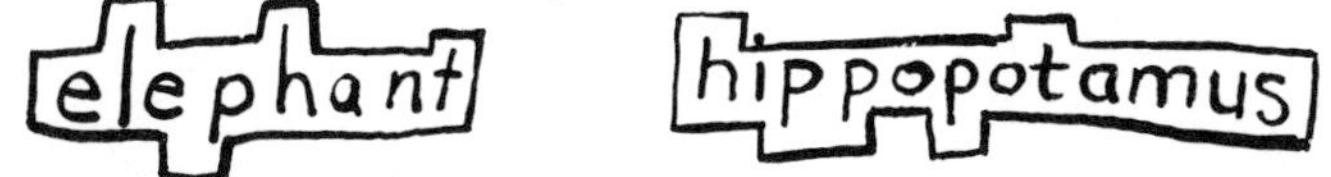

Sometimes a primary-grade teacher prints a word on the chalkboard and asks the child to place his hands on either side of the word to emphasize its total shape. The framing of words also is an example of the use of word form clues. Even words that first must be analyzed using another word recognition technique eventually become part of a reader's stock of sight words, and he then recognizes them as a whole.

FIGURE 1-3

Phonetic analysis is recognizing a word by associating the sounds in a word with the symbols that stand for them. Phonetic analysis is most useful in analyzing words which are phonetically regular so they can be sounded and blended without any difficulty. Structural analysis consists of the use of word parts that are blended into whole words. Structural analysis, therefore, is composed of the subskills of the use of base or root words, prefixes, suffixes, syllabication, compound words, and contractions.

Picture clues enable a reader to recognize a word by associating it with the picture that it stands for. Picture clues mainly are used in the beginning stages of reading instruction. Context clues enable a reader to arrive at the meaning of an unknown word by using the words around it such as the other words in a sentence, paragraph, or passage. Context clues are very useful if they are combined with simple phonetic analysis such as the use of the initial consonant sound. Dictionary usage deals with getting the meaning or pronunciation of a word by using a dictionary or a book glossary.

A reader must be efficient in word recognition to be able to go on to the next more complex part of the reading process—association.

Association

The next more complex part of the reading process is usually called association and deals with a reader's associating the symbols that he is reading with the experiences that they represent. As an example, the word "snow" simply is a visual representation of snow, and a reader must know what snow looks like to be able to fully understand the word "snow" when he is reading about it. Therefore, an efficient reader must have many experiences, ideas, and concepts to draw upon or he cannot understand what he is reading.

Therefore, it is very important for a teacher to be sure that each child she is teaching has adequate experiences and concepts to associate with the symbols that he is reading. A wide background of experiences is *especially* important either for a culturally disadvantaged or slow-learning child. If a disadvantaged child or any child has not had any of the experiences that he is reading about, he cannot associate them with the symbols that they stand for.

Comprehension

Comprehension or understanding what is read often is considered to be the third part of the reading process. Comprehension is built upon both word recognition and association and cannot effectively take place unless the reader first is efficient in these two aspects of reading. Reading without comprehension is not reading but rather is mere verbalism or "word calling." A child may be able to pronounce all of the words in a passage correctly, but if he is unable to understand what he is reading, the pronunciation of the words is not reading.

There are several levels of comprehension in reading—a literal level and a higher-type level. The lower level of comprehension usually is called literal comprehension and deals with reproducing or translating an author's words while answering a question based upon what was read. Higher-type comprehension sometimes is called inferential comprehension and consists of reading between the lines or understanding the implied meanings in what is read. Inferential comprehension also consists of the drawing of conclusions and generalizations, sensing the author's mood and purpose, and predicting outcomes. Higher-type comprehension questions always involve a reader's thinking about his answer in some way.

Effective comprehension also requires that a reader be able to sense the relation between the various words in a sentence, between the sentences in a paragraph, and between the paragraphs in a passage. Comprehension also deals with the science of semantics, or the multiple meanings that words can have. Many less precise words in the English language contain many meanings, and their meaning changes depending upon how they are used in a sentence. As an example, the word "cut" has 108 meanings according to one dictionary. It is obvious that the reader must choose the correct meaning of the word "cut" as it is used in the sentence that he is reading if he is to have effective comprehension. A more precise word such as "parallel" usually has only one meaning no matter what context it is used in.

Evaluating What Is Read

A number of reading specialists consider evaluating what is read, or critical reading, to be the next higher level of the reading process. Critical reading is dependent upon good word recognition techniques, and effectiveness in both association and comprehension. Some reading specialists consider critical reading to be the highest level of inferential comprehension, but in this book evaluating what is read is considered to be another part of the reading process.

Critical reading mainly conists of a reader's evaluating what he is reading in terms of some objective criteria. It also can include the understanding of different propaganda techniques. Critical reading is based upon critical thinking since reading is a thinking process.

Evaluating can be begun as early as the reading readiness level when a child critically interprets a picture in a tradebook or in a reading readiness workbook such as finding an obvious mistake in a picture. Children in the primary grades can answer critical questions effectively if the questions are kept within the background of their experiences. However, critical reading usually is more emphasized beginning in the intermediate grades and continuing into secondary school and college.

Evaluating what is read probably is best developed in children by the teacher's often asking questions which call for critical answers. Children are required to think critically when their teacher has asked them a question which calls for a critical or evaluative response. It also can be developed by having a child read several books to find the answer to the same question. Units as are taught in social studies, in science, and the use of the newspaper also are good for developing critical reading.

Children usually will not develop critical reading ability even if they are otherwise very good readers unless teachers make special efforts to ask questions calling for critical answers and encourage a questioning attitude in classroom activities. It is, of course, absolutely essential that critical reading be taught well to all elementary-school children since the success of a democracy depends upon citizens who can react objectively and critically to what they read.

The Use of Reading for Problem-Solving

The highest level of the reading process consists of a reader's use of the knowledge that he has gained from reading in his own life in some way. The use of reading for problem-solving usually is called creative or integrative reading. This highest level of reading depends upon a reader's effectiveness in word recognition techniques, association, and comprehension.

Creative reading really is the ultimate goal of all reading instruction, and each teacher should help all of the children she teaches to reach this level of the reading process. Creative reading can be used as early as first grade when a child makes something as a result of his reading. It also can be used with disabled readers early in a corrective reading program when a child constructs something like an airplane model after reading how to do it.

This level of reading can involve bibliotherapy, the solving of a personal problem by reading about it. Bibliotherapy often can be used effectively with a disabled reader. If such a child reads about a child who has a similar personal problem, he often may be helped to solve this personal problem.

Evaluating reading instruction at this level is very difficult since there are no standardized reading tests that even attempt to measure it. The results of reading instruction at the creative level sometimes may not be known by a teacher for many years. However, even though the use of reading for problem-solving is difficult to evaluate effectively, it is the level toward which all teachers should point both good and disabled readers.

The Teaching of Reading

Since the reading process is composed of the interrelated and cumulative factors of eye movements, word recognition, association, comprehension, critical reading, and creative reading, it is important that every teacher emphasize all of these aspects for each child that she is teaching in spite of his lack of reading ability. Therefore, to teach reading effectively both to good and disabled readers, the teacher cannot just emphasize word recognition, but also must consider the teaching of comprehension, critical reading, and creative reading. Often all of these aspects of reading can be presented at basically the same stage of either a developmental or corrective reading program.

Certainly it is the right of every child in our democratic society to receive instruction in each of these parts of the reading process and to reach the maximum level of which he is capable in each of its dimensions.

SUMMARY

In this chapter reading was described as being a very complex process with several interrelated and cumulative parts. The eye movements which take place while a person is reading is the first part of the reading process. An improvement in the eye movements usually takes place along with any improvement that occurs in reading itself as a result of a person's reading much easy material in which he is interested. The second part of reading consists of the word recognition techniques of word form clues, phonetic analysis, structural analysis, picture and context clues, and dictionary usage. Skill in word recognition is absolutely essential if a person is to be an effective reader, but the mere pronunciation or recognition of words is not true reading, but rather is verbalism.

Next a reader must associate the visual symbols which he sees with the experiences that they represent. Comprehension or understanding of what is read usually is considered to be the next phase of reading, and reading without comprehension is not reading. There are several levels of comprehension—a literal level and a higher-type level. For effective comprehension, a reader must not only understand the meaning of single words, but also must be able to sense the relation between the words in a sentence, between the sentences in a paragraph, and between the paragraphs in a passage.

Evaluating what is read, critical reading, is sometimes considered to be the next part of the reading process. Critical reading can be developed as early as the primary grades, and much direct instruction is needed if children are to become critical readers. Of course, good critical reading ability is an absolute necessity in a democracy. The highest level of reading is the use of the knowledges and attitudes gained from reading for problem-solving. This level of reading is called creative or integrative reading and is the level toward which all reading instruction should be pointed.

In working with disabled readers, the teacher may begin with word recognition, but she should also be sure that comprehension of what is read always is emphasized. Very soon critical and creative reading should be presented even to disabled readers. Each child needs to achieve competence in all areas of reading.

REFERENCES

Hildreth, Gertrude. *Teaching Reading.* New York: Holt, Rinehart and Winston Incorporated, 1958. Chapter 4.

Spache, George and Evelyn B. Spache. *Reading in the Elementary School.* Boston: Allyn and Bacon, Incorporated, 1969. Chapter 1.

Strang, Ruth, Constance McCullough, and Arthur E. Traxler. *The Improvement of Reading.* New York: McGraw-Hill Book Company, 1967. Chapter 1.

2

Determining the Major Causes of Individual Reading Difficulties

There can be many causes for both minor and severe reading disabilities. This chapter discusses the more common causes of reading problems and illustrates some ways in which the causes of reading difficulties can be determined as much as is possible. In this chapter the following causes of reading problems found in elementary schools are discussed: the lack of sufficient readiness before beginning formal reading instruction, inadequate or improper reading instruction in the elementary school, various physical defects, inadequate language development and speech defects, an inadequate level of intelligence, directional difficulties, incompletely developed neurological dominance, dyslexia, and social-emotional maladjustment.

The chapter also emphasizes the multiple causation theory of reading disability and shows how there is rarely only one cause for a child's reading problems.

Inadequate Readiness Before Formal Reading Instruction

One very common cause for reading disability in elementary-school children is the lack of sufficient reading readiness before formal instruction. This is especially true for immature and slow-learning children. At the beginning of the school year every first-grade classroom contains several immature children who really should not be in first grade. These children usually are of normal or even above average intelligence but just are immature either physically or emotionally. Probably such children should not have entered kindergarten at the time that they did or they should have been kept in kindergarten for a second year.

However, if they are placed in first grade, the teacher should *not* begin any kind of formal reading instruction with them until she judges them ready to read by using a standardized reading readiness test, visual and auditory discrimination tests, and careful teacher observation. Instead of formal reading instruction for such children, an informal reading readiness program should be used which might consist of the provision of many kinds of experiences, the use of the language-experience approach, and the use of some reading readiness workbook pages or teacher-made worksheets. Often this development of adequate reading readiness may take from six weeks to several months, but it certainly will be very well worth the time and effort spent on it.

On the other hand, if immature children are given a formal reading program before they are really ready, they are *very* likely to fail in it almost as soon as it begins. Since the learning of the reading skills is so orderly, such children begin to fall farther and farther behind as new reading skills are presented which are based upon the reading skills that they already have failed to learn. As such children begin to fail in reading, they develop a dislike for it and a poor self-concept which makes it even more difficult for them to succeed in reading. Thus they become disabled readers in first grade and often remain disabled readers for the rest of their lives unless they receive special reading instruction. However, it is so much easier to prevent reading difficulties rather than to have to correct them.

The teacher can often discover if a disabled reader's reading problems are caused by the lack of sufficient readiness before formal reading instruction by noticing from the school records just when his reading problems began. If the school records show that the child's disability began in first grade, it is quite likely that it is the result of inadequate readiness. The teacher of a disabled reader also can check with the child's kindergarten and first-grade teachers or with the comments of these teachers in his folder to see if his teachers believed that he was immature.

Inadequate or Improper Reading Instruction

Many cases of reading problems in the elementary school are caused by either inadequate or improper reading instruction especially in the early primary grades. Many school personnel are not happy to acknowledge this since they believe it reflects unfavorably on them, but it must be accepted as a fact. This is not to imply that elementary schools always have had much control over all of the factors in school which cause reading difficulties, but school personnel must accept the responsibility anyway.

At the present time, elementary schools in America are staffed by too many teachers who just do not understand the reading process well enough to be able to teach it effectively. They do not have sufficient knowledge of reading to be able to effectively diagnose or correct either the word recognition or comprehension difficulties of the children in their classrooms, probably especially the word recognition difficulties. Teachers can be found in elementary schools who have not had a single reading course for many years. Also some of the beginning teachers have had very inadequate undergraduate reading methods courses which really have not prepared them for teaching reading. A number of these courses are too theoretical, and the undergraduate students do not have enough actual contact with children in these courses. Sometimes secondary school teachers or liberal arts graduates who have not had one course in the teaching of elementary reading are placed in primary-grade classrooms.

Especially in the past, many elementary schools have been unwilling to let children progress in reading at their own rate and read on their own level. Instead, administrators and teachers have accepted the grade level designation of each basal reader as the reading level at which each child in that elementary class should read no matter what his actual reading ability might be. Not only has this practice held the better readers back, but even more important it has caused the children in the slow reading group to continually read at their frustration level, one or more years above their actual reading level. When a child is forced to continually read at the frustration level, he never can experience success in reading and soon becomes a disabled reader.

In the past and to some extent at the present a number of schools have adopted one reading method for use with all children in an elementary classroom in spite of their special reading needs and abilities. As an example, sometimes a formal phonics program is used with all elementary-school children in a classroom even if some of them do not have good auditory discrimination (the ability to hear likenesses and differences in words), do not have adequate auditory acuity (hearing ability), or adequate mental age to learn to read by a formal phonics program. On the other hand, some children who do not have adequate visual perception (the ability to discriminate visually between letters and words) cannot learn to read effectively through a visual or sight method and have not received enough training in phonetic analysis. In addition, the few children who can learn to read best by a kinesthetic (tactile or VAKT) method have not had any training at all of this kind. The reading teacher should be knowledgeable about many different reading methods so that she can choose the best one to use with any individual child either in the regular classroom or in the reading improvement program.

There also have been some school-related reading difficulties which the school cannot really be held responsible for. Frequent illnesses or many absences in first grade or in the later primary grades can greatly contribute to subsequent reading difficulty. When a child goes to another elementary school, particularly one in which the reading method used is quite different, he can experience difficulty with reading. As an example, if a child has been in a first grade in which the initial teaching alphabet is used and he moves to a school in which the basal reader approach is used, he can be very confused about reading for a long time. During this period of confusion, he can become disabled in reading since the skills must be learned in an orderly manner.

Very large classes, especially in the primary grades, can significantly contribute to reading difficulties. No primary-grade classroom should really contain more than twenty-five children, while a classroom of twenty children is much better for the teaching of reading since instruction can then be more individualized. However, a number of primary-grade classrooms contain more than thirty or even thirty-five children. No intermediate-grade classroom should have more than thirty children, while twenty-five children is much better. A number of intermediate-grade classrooms also can be found with more than thirty children.

Another school-related cause of reading disability that cannot really be called the responsibility of the school is the inability of some teachers to decide just how to motivate different children to make reading improvement. As an example, a number of children make the best progress in reading when their teacher provides a warm, permissive classroom environment and treats them kindly, removing most of the pressure for learning to read. Many children respond best to this type of teacher and school environment. On the other hand, a few children need a much firmer teacher who will command their respect since they need pressure to apply themselves to reading in the way that they should.

It is very difficult to tell a teacher how she should deal with the different children in her classroom since she really has to sense this herself. This aspect of teaching behavior has not received much research up to this time because it is very difficult to define a teacher-pupil relationship objectively. However, the teacher-pupil relationship should be considered when thinking about school-related reading disability.

It probably is difficult for a teacher to determine if a disabled reader has difficulty in reading due to a school-caused reason. The teacher probably would know if it is the policy of the school to use the grade level designation of the basal readers as the reading level of all children in any elementary classroom. This also is true of the use of one method of reading instruction for all children in an elementary classroom. The cumulative record of a child may give the teacher an indication of his attendance record and if he has changed schools a number of times, especially in the primary grades. There may be no way to determine if a disabled reader was placed in a very large classroom unless the teacher knows of the school's policy on this matter. The teacher may get some indication of the way a teacher in the past has viewed the disabled reader by talking to her or by looking at the anecdotal comments in the child's folder.

Various Physical Causes

There usually are considered to be three main physical causes of reading disability in the elementary school, not including incompletely developed neurological dominance which is usually thought of as a separate cause. The three physical causes for reading problems which are discussed in this section are visual defects, auditory defects, and an endocrine malfunction.

Visual defects are not as common a cause of reading difficulties as most people believe. Adequate vision usually is necessary for successful reading since a reader must see the words visually before recognizing them or before associating them with past experiences, but children sometimes can be good readers with inadequate vision.

A child in first grade must have adequate near-point vision to be able to see the printed words on the page. Sometimes the eye muscles are not finely enough developed to allow children to have adequate near-point vision for reading when they enter first grade. Usually these eye muscles do develop later, but reading disability can result in first grade if children are asked to do much book reading before they are visually ready in this way. The teacher can identify children with inadequate near-point vision by noticing which children complain of difficulty in seeing the words on the printed pages in their books. For such children a beginning reading program which makes much use of the chalkboard or large lined sheets of paper is very good. The use of language-experience charts, therefore, is very effective with such children in a beginning reading program.

Another visual defect which can cause reading disability is the lack of fusion of the two eyes of a child. When any reader looks at a printed page, he sees two images, and his eyes must be able to fuse or join these two images into one image if he is to be able to see the printed words clearly. The lack of binocular coordination or fusion normally occurs in young children, and often can be corrected by a child's doing eye exercises that an opthomologist (eye specialist) recommends. Binocular fusion can be tested by using the Massachusetts Vision Test and the Keystone Visual Survey Telebinocular.[1]

There are really two kinds of visual defects which commonly are found in elementary-school children. One of these is hyperopia (farsightedness) and the other is myopia (nearsightedness). Hyperopia sometimes can be a cause of reading disability although probably it is not a cause as often as is sometimes thought. The farsighted child has some difficulty with near-point reading such as is required in reading a book, but often he can read the chalkboard

[1]"The Massachusetts Vision Test," Welch-Allen Company, Auburn, New York: "The Keystone Visual Survey Telebinocular." The Keystone Company, Meadville, Pennsylvania.

well enough. Hyperopia is not very common among children in the elementary school but is more common among adults.

Nearsightedness is more common among elementary-school children, but is rarely related to reading disability since myopic children can see a printed page adequately although they may have to hold the book quite close to their face to be able to do so. They do have difficulty with written instructions that have been placed on the chalkboard. Myopic children often are very good readers in the elementary school if their visual problem has been corrected with eye glasses.

The old Snellen Chart really is not adequate for judging vision for reading instruction since it tests a child's sight at far-point instead of at near-point such as is needed in reading a book. However, vision can be adequately tested at school by the school nurse or by a specially trained parent by using the illuminated Snellen Chart (supplemented by tests of muscular imbalance and depth perception). The School Vision Tester, The Massachusetts Vison Test, or The Keystone Visual Survey Telebinocular.[2] Most of these tests judge vision at near-point, judge depth perception, and evaluate binocular coordination.

The teacher also can gain a clue to possible vision problems in disabled readers by using the "A-B-C's" of vision. These are as follows: (a) the appearance of the eyes—the redness, the watering of the eyes, and frequent sties; (b) the behavior of the child—signs of nervousness, how far the book is held away from the eyes, and the posture of the body; and (c) the complaints of the child such as frequent headaches, seeing double, blurring of the printed page, and nausea.[3]

Auditory defects also can be a cause of reading disability, but probably are somewhat less related than are visual defects. Hearing loss especially may be related to reading problems if a formal phonics method is used which requires a child to hear the

---

[2]See: Sweeting, Orville J., "An Improved Vision Screening Program for the New Haven Schools: A Case History," *Journal of the American Optometric Association,* 30, May, 1959, pp. 715-722: "The School Vision Tester," Bausch and Lomb, Rochester, New York: "The Massachusetts Vision Test," Welch-Allen Company, Auburn, New York; "The Keystone Visual Survey Telebinocular," The Keystone Company, Meadville, Pennsylvania.

[3]Lois B. Bing, "Children's Vision and School Success," The Committee on Visual Problems of Children and Youth of the American Optometric Association, St. Louis, Missouri.

differences between phonemes (sounds), between consonant blends, between consonant digraphs, or between diphthongs. Auditory discrimination (the ability to hear the likenesses and differences between sounds in words) is related to success in beginning reading, again especially if some sort of formal phonics program is used.

Hearing loss also can lead to speech defects which in turn can be related to reading problems. If a child has some hearing loss, a predominantly visual method in which words are taught by sight as a whole, a kinesthetic method which involves the tracing of syllables, or both methods in combination can be used, and the child should be taught to rely on the word recognition skill of phonetic analysis as little as possible. Even totally deaf children can learn to read effectively if the proper method is used with them.

The classroom teacher can test a child's auditory acuity (hearing ability) by holding a loudly ticking watch about 48 inches from the child's ear and then slowly withdrawing the watch and writing down the distance when the child no longer hears the ticking of the watch. However, the teacher should remember that this test is not scientifically valid, but must be used only as an indicator of a child's possible hearing loss. The school nurse can give a very valid hearing test by using an audiometer, an instrument designed to test auditory acuity very accurately. A hearing test on an audiometer can be given individually or to an entire class at the same time by using the Western Electric Company's Model 4C audiometer.

An endocrine malfunction is caused when a gland of the body such as the pituitary gland or the thyroid gland does not function properly. This is a rare cause of reading problems, but sometimes an elementary teacher may see a child with hypothyroidism, which means that his thyroid gland does not function as it should. Hypothyroidism makes a child act sluggish and therefore he may be unable to profit from reading instruction as much as he should. On the other hand, hyperthyroidism occurs when the thyroid gland functions too much. A child with hyperthyroidism is overactive and therefore may not be able to concentrate on reading instruction as much as he might. Malfunctions of the thyroid gland usually can be corrected by proper medication. A pituitary dysfunction may cause reversal tendencies, poor motor coordination, or mental retardation.

Many kinds of chronic illnesses such as asthma, frequent colds, tonsilitis, or diabetes can cause frequent school absences which can lead to reading problems because of missed reading instruction. Since reading must be learned in a developmental manner, missed instruction at many stages of reading can lead to reading disability.

The teacher can tell much about possible physical causes for reading disability by observation, as was indicated earlier in this section. The teacher also can look at the child's health records to determine if in the past he has had vision, auditory, or some other type of physical defect which may account at least in part for his present reading problem.

Inadequate Language Development and Speech Defects

Good oral language ability is one of the most predictive factors of good primary-grade reading achievement. A child with good oral language ability speaks in complete and complex sentences, uses a varied and precise vocabulary, uses many descriptive words such as adjectives and adverbs, and uses correct grammar. Chapter 9 describes how a child's oral language is learned in the home through imitation of his parents and older brothers and sisters. Inadequate language development can be a cause of reading difficulty although probably often it is one of several causes for a child. It may be a fairly important cause of reading problems either for culturally disadvantaged children, bilingual children, or for slow-learning children.

Culturally disadvantaged children often speak in a restricted language style, which means that they use short simple sentences, imprecise vocabulary, few adjectives and adverbs, and incorrect grammar. Therefore, in school they sometimes have difficulty in understanding their teacher's language when she is giving reading instruction orally. They also sometimes have difficulty in reading the language patterns found in most basal readers.

Obviously, a bilingual child or one who speaks some language other than English in his home, is likely to have difficulty in school reading for many of the same reasons. He cannot understand his teacher's language and is therfore unable to profit from reading instruction. He also has difficulty both in asking his teacher questions about reading instruction and in answering her comprehension questions about what is read. The bilingual child also has difficulty in reading orally. Perhaps, most importantly, he cannot understand the language patterns found in the basal readers. The bilingual child really needs to learn how to *speak* English effectively before he can learn to read it.

Slow-learning children very often have inadequate language development, and mental retardation usually is best indicated by a slow oral language development. Slow-learning children also use short, simple sentences and very few descriptive words. Their vocabulary development is very limited. Therefore, such children often have difficulty in understanding the language of their teacher and in interpreting the language patterns used in basal reader stories.

Speech defects such as improper articulation, lisping, or stuttering may be related to reading problems. However, speech defects probably are not a very common cause of reading disability. If a child cannot articulate or say the sounds in words in exactly the way which his teacher does, he may have difficulty with word recognition especially in the area of phonetic analysis.

A child also may drop the endings of words such as saying "in'" for "ing." Therefore, such a child may have difficulty with structural analysis. If a child stutters, he probably will dislike reading orally and will be deficient at least in this area of reading. A child who stutters also may develop a poor self-concept which will make it more difficult for him to learn to read effectively.

The teacher who decides that inadequate language development has contributed to a disabled reader's reading problem can do so either as a result of observing him while he is talking or by examining his previous teachers' comments which can be found in his cumulative folder. Speech defects can be observed by the teacher while listening to the disabled reader speak or by looking at his folder to see if he has had speech correction in the past.

An Inadequate Level of Intelligence

Slow-learning children in first grade are *not* ready to read at the beginning of the year since it has been fairly well accepted by reading specialists that a mental age of about six and a half is needed for success in most formal beginning reading programs. It is also believed that a mental age of at least seven and a half is necessary for success in beginning phonetic analysis. When the formula 1Q=MA/CAX100 is used, it can be seen a child with an intelligence quotient of less than 100 does not reach the mental age of six and a half until he is older than six and a half chronologically.

By using this formula, it can be seen that a child with an intelligence quotient of 80 does not reach the mental age of six and one half until he is a little more than eight years old chronologically. The child with an IQ of 80 is considered to be a slow-learning child since such a child normally has an IQ ranging from 70 to 90. The child with an intelligence quotient of 80 has advanced 0.8 of a year intellectually for each year of chronological life.

Therefore, the child with an intelligence quotient of 80 should not really receive formal reading instruction until he is almost in third grade. Practically speaking, this will not happen in any school in the near future, even in an ungraded primary classroom, because all parents expect their child to receive formal reading instruction almost as soon as they enter school. However, an extended reading readiness period lasting for at least half of first grade or more will be of some help in preventing reading difficulties for slow-learning children.

A reading readiness program emphasizing visual discrimination by using teacher-made visual discrimination worksheets, the pages from reading readiness workbooks that emphasize visual discrimination, or the Frostig Program for the Development of Visual Perception[4] can be very useful for slow-learning children. Many kinds of auditory discrimination activities such as listening to the sounds found on special records, rhyming activities, listening to nursery rhymes and poems, and looking at objects beginning with the same sounds can be useful in developing readiness for these children. Many kinds of experiences such as school trips to interesting places, the use of the language-experience approach, and working with manipulative materials such as crayons, drawing paper, clay, scissors, paste and paints also can be good for slow-learning children.

An inadequate level of intelligence really is not a cause of primary-grade reading disability if the child has sufficient readiness

---

[4]Marianne Frostig and David Horne, *The Frostig Program for Visual Perception* (Chicago: Follett Publishing Company, 1964).

before beginning a reading program, and if the program is sequentially organized with much concrete and meaningful repetition. At the beginning stages of reading, prior experiences are more important than is intellectual ability. However, by the intermediate grades, intelligence is important in reading success due to the abstract thinking which is required in higher-type comprehension. Slow-learning children do have difficulty with abstract thinking and do much better in activities requiring concrete thinking. Therefore, a lack of intellectual ability can be a cause of reading disability. However, most slow-learning children *can* learn to read well enough to succeed in the modern world if they have proper instruction and good motivation to learn to read.

Many slow-learning children already are overachieving in the elementary school, and therefore special reading instruction can do them no great good. As an example, a child with an intelligence quotient of 80 in the fourth grade who is reading near the end of the second grade reading level probably is doing as well as is expected, while the child in fourth grade with an IQ of 80 who is reading at the upper third grade level is already overachieving.

The teacher can determine if a child is a slow-learner by examining the intelligence test results which are found in his cumulative folder. If his IQ ranges from 70 to 90, he is thought of as slow learning, while an IQ of 90 to 100 indicates that he is somewhat below average. However, the test results from both group intelligence tests or individual intelligence tests cannot be thought of as being free from error. Any group intelligence test yields a score which is less reliable than that found on an individual intelligence test such as the Wechsler Intelligence Scale for Children (WISC) or the Stanford-Binet Intelligence Scale. A listing of both group and individual intelligence tests is found in Chapter 4. The teacher can also often determine if a child is slow-learning by observing him as he performs various tasks in the classroom.

Directional Difficulties

Directional difficulties are a fairly uncommon cause of reading disability in the elementary school. However, a few children do have directional difficulties which means that they are likely to reverse either letter, words, or even entire sentences. As an example, a child with a directional difficulty often reverses the letters "b" and "d" or "p" and "q" and can reverse the words "stop" and "spot" or "was" and "saw." Some children with a directional difficulty are mirror writers, meaning that they start writing on the right-hand side of the page and then write from right to left, reversing the entire sentence, the words within the sentence, and the letters within the words. Their writing can only be read when it is held up to a mirror.

Reversals are often caused because the right side of a child's brain is dominant, which in turn makes the child left-handed. Therefore, both children who have occasional reversals and mirror writers usually are left-handed children. Sometimes mixed dominance, happening when neither of the two sides of the brain is totally dominant, also can cause reversals. As an example, a child with mixed dominance may be right-eyed, left-handed, and right-footed. Most children with reversals, even those who are mirror writers, overcome this tendency without special help by the time they are in the later primary or early intermediate grades.

The teacher probably can best determine a child with directional difficulties by observation of his writing and reading. She can examine his writing to see if he has reversed either letters within words or entire words while writing them. She also can observe his oral reading to see if he commonly reverses words while reading them. The teacher also may examine the child's cumulative folder to see if directional difficulties have been a problem for him in the past. Of course, she can determine if he has mixed dominance by observing which eye he closes when he is practicing archery or sighting a rifle, which hand he uses when throwing a ball or when writing, and which foot he uses to lead with when he is walking. The teacher can also use the Harris Tests for Lateral Dominance to determine if a disabled reader has established or mixed lateral dominance.[5]

Incompletely Developed Neurological Dominance

Another possible cause of reading disability which is quite related to directional difficulties is incompletely developed neurological dominance. The human brain contains two hemispheres

---

[5] "Harris Tests for Lateral Dominance," Psychological Corporation, New York.

or sides, and in most children one hemisphere of the brain becomes dominant by the time they are five or six years old. If the left side of a person's brain is dominant, he will be right-eyed, right-handed, and right-footed. On the other hand, a person whose right side of the brain is dominant will be left-eyed, left-handed, and left-footed. According to a theory stated by Carl Delacato and Glenn Doman, both of the Institute for the Development of Human Potential in Philadelphia, most language and reading disabilities are caused by incompletely established neurological dominance when neither hemisphere of the brain has established dominance. This is somewhat different from mixed dominance, but it does contain many of the same elements.

To prevent and correct incompletely established dominance, Delacato and Doman have developed a method for establishing dominance which is described in Chapter 9. Most reading specialists do not believe that incompletely developed lateral dominance is a very common cause of reading problems. It probably instead is just one contributing cause that sometimes occurs along with several other causes.

The teacher can determine if a young child has established lateral dominance by noticing if he uses the same hand all the time when he is eating, writing, drawing, or throwing a ball. If he seems to use either hand, he probably has not established dominance. Most children do establish dominance firmly by the time they are about six years old. The teacher can look at the child's folder to see if there are teacher comments about incompletely established dominance when the child was younger. The Harris Tests for Lateral Dominance which were mentioned earlier in this section can also be used with young children to see if they have firmly established dominance.

Dyslexia

Another possible cause of reading disability is dyslexia, which is defined as specific reading disability caused by a minimal brain dysfunction. Children with dyslexia have a minor brain dysfunction, but neurologists as yet are not just sure in what way the brain does not function properly.

A child with dyslexia is unable to learn to read very effectively. The teacher may teach him a word which he learns and then forgets several minutes later. He just cannot seem to hold either the visual or the auditory image of the word in his mind. Often the child with dyslexia is hyperactive and distractable.

Dyslexia or specific reading disability is not as common a cause of reading problems as is sometimes said. Many reading specialists state that less than five percent of all disabled readers in the elementary school have dyslexia. There are special methods for treating a dyslexic child which will be described in Chapter 5. Both the Gillingham-Stillman Method and the Fernald Method can be used in the treatment of dyslexia.

The teacher may assume through observation that a disabled reader has dyslexia when he is unable to retain the visual or auditory representations of words even though he is of normal intelligence. The report of a neurologist can be helpful in determining if a child really has dyslexia, but even this cannot be considered a sure indication. Since it is so difficult to determine if a child really has dyslexia and since this is a medical term, the teacher should never label a disabled reader as a dyslexic unless she is absolutely certain of this fact.

Social-Emotional Maladjustment

The beginning stages of reading require that a first-grade child have a number of personality characteristics. Success in beginning reading normally requires a child who is curious, emotionally mature, responsible, and able to follow directions. If a child does not have one or even several of these characteristics, it does not mean that he necessarily will become a disabled reader in school. However, a child does need to have most of these personal characteristics to be successful in reading.

If a child is not well adjusted before he enters school, this may cause reading problems in school. However, usually a poor emotional adjustment upon entering school is a fairly rare cause of reading disability. Most children enter school very much wanting to learn to read and only later become emotionally disturbed if they do not learn to read as well as they think they should. Such emotional maladjustment occurs because learning to read well is a very important developmental task for all children. Most often, emotional maladjustment and reading problems form a reciprocal relationship in which a slight emotional maladjustment leads to reading problems which later lead to more severe emotional maladjustment. This relationship becomes a vicious circle which is very difficult to break.

A few children do not want to learn to read either when they enter school or when they are placed in a special reading program because being unable to read satisfies a number of their needs. Not being able to read may enable them to remain dependent on their parents and to not grow up and accept responsibility. Sometimes not being able to read allows a child to punish his parents in a subtle way for things that happen to him in the home.

In school, disabled readers can display many different kinds of behavior. They can be passive, withdrawn, disinterested, and uncaring about all school activities. On the other hand, some disabled readers are aggressive, hostile, and destructive. Most disabled readers have some degree of emotional maladjustment as the result of their inability to read, something which both their parents and society require that they must learn to do at school. Sometimes disabled readers must receive special therapy from a psychologist or a psychiatrist before a reading improvement program can be begun, but usually a program of reading improvement on a child's reading level emphasizing only those reading skills which he needs and taught by an understanding teacher will help him solve his emotional problems.

Therefore, emotional maladjustment probably rarely is the sole cause of reading disability in the elementary school. Instead, emotional problems usually are a contributing cause along with several other causes for reading problems. Much of the time the emotional maladjustment resulting from reading disability will disappear when the reading problem is corrected.

A teacher can try to determine the relation between a disabled reader's emotional maladjustment and his reading difficulty in a number of different ways. She can talk both to the child himself about his reading problem and to his parents about what they believe may be the causes for the problem. She also can examine the child's cumulative folder and notice the comments about his emotional adjustment which were written by his previous teachers. Obviously, the help of the school social worker, an elementary guidance counselor, psychologist, or psychiatrist also can be enlisted. One of these specialists or at times the teacher herself can use a projective technique with the disabled reader, such as the Goodenough Draw-a-Man Test, the House-Tree-Person Test, the Incomplete Sentences Test, the Three Wishes Test, the Children's Apperception Test (CAT), or the Blacky Test. A discussion about some projective techniques is found in Chapter 3.

The Multiple Causation Theory of Reading Disability

There rarely is one single cause for reading problems. Instead, the multiple causation theory of reading disability has been well accepted by reading specialists for many years. Since reading is a very complex process consisting of the visual aspects, association, comprehension, and creative reading, it follows that there often are several causes for any one case of reading disability.

As an example, in many cases a primary cause for reading disability such as inadequate readiness before formal reading instruction is compounded by the emotional maladjustment which results from early failure in reading. This also is true when a child does not learn to read effectively because of inadequate or improper reading instruction and emotional problems result. Usually some of the causes of reading disability will disappear, such as emotional maladjustment, when the child has made reading improvement.

It is important for either the classroom teacher or the special reading teacher to try if possible to determine the exact causes of a disabled reader's reading problems. It is possible and desirable for a teacher to treat the symptoms of reading disability while she is trying to discover the exact causes for the reading problem. However, she should make an effort to set up some hypotheses or ideas as to why the child has a problem. These hypotheses or hunches should be tentative and subject to change as the teacher gains more information through a number of ways such as by observation, talking with the child and his parents, testing, and examining school records. Chapter 3 describes some commonly used standardized and informal reading tests which can be used to determine both the reading problem and, to an extent, its causes.

As was indicated earlier, often the disabled reader himself can give reasons for his reading problem. The teacher also can gain clues to the causes of the child's reading disability by talking to his parents or to his former teachers. Sometimes projective techniques which are discussed in Chapter 3 also are useful in determing the causes of reading problems. In any case, the teacher should be aware of the fact that there are many causes of reading disability, and that they usually operate in combination.

SUMMARY

This chapter described the most common causes for the reading problems which are found in the elementary school. One of the more common causes of reading disability is the lack of sufficient readiness before formal reading instruction in first grade. It is especially important that immature and slow-learning children be given a sufficient period of reading readiness activities to insure that they are really ready for reading.

Another very common cause of reading difficulty is inadequate or improper reading instruction in the elementary school. Many teachers do not understand the complex reading process well enough to be able to teach it effectively, nor are they able to diagnose and correct minor reading difficulties as they occur. They also are not able to individualize reading instruction by using the appropriate methods and materials.

There are three main physical causes for reading problems, all of which are somewhat related. Visual problems which are related to reading are mainly the lack of binocular fusion and hyperopia (farsightedness). Reading problems can result from poor auditory discrimination, inadequate auditory memory, or some degree of hearing loss especially when a formal method is used. Endocrine malfunction is a rare cause of reading disability which results from sluggish behavior due to the underfunctioning of the thyroid gland.

Oral language ability is highly related to reading success, and particularly culturally disadvantaged and slow-learning children may have poor oral language ability due to an improper language model in the home or their lack of mental ability. Speech defects may be related to reading disability especially when a formal phonics program is used.

Intellectual ability is related to reading success usually beginning in the intermediate grades. However, a slow-learning child cannot be considered a disabled reader if he is reading up to the level of his capacity. Slow-learning children do have difficulty with the abstract thinking required in higher-type comprehension.

Directional difficulties and incompletely developed lateral dominance may have some relation to reading problems, but this has not been firmly established by research. Directional difficulties can cause reversals which normally disappear by the time a child reaches the later primary or early intermediate grades.

Dyslexia is a specific reading disability caused by a minimal brain dysfunction in which a child has great difficulty remembering words either by visual or auditory means. Dyslexic children are very rare in an elementary school.

The relation between emotional maladjustment and reading problems is very clear. Usually reading problems cause emotional maladjustment which in turn leads to further reading disability. Very often emotional problems disappear when the child makes reading improvement. Occasionally a child comes to school with such a severe emotional problem which he has developed at home that he cannot learn to read. Such a child usually has to have therapy from a professional person before he can profit from either developmental or corrective reading instruction.

The multiple causation theory of reading disability is accepted by most reading specialists. This theory states that there usually are several causes for reading problems which are operating in combination.

REFERENCES

Bond, Guy L. and Miles A. Tinker. *Reading Difficulties: Their Diagnosis and Correction.* New York: Appleton-Century-Crofts, 1967. Chapters 5 and 6.

Carter, Homer L. J. and Dorothy J. McGinnis. *Diagnosis and Treatment of the Disabled Reader.* New York: The Macmillan Company, 1970. Chapter 4.

Dechant, Emerald. *Diagnosis and Remediation of Reading Disability.* West Nyack, New York: Parker Publishing Company, 1968, Chapter 3.

Strang, Ruth. *Reading Diagnosis and Remediation.* Newark, Delaware: IRA Research Fund, 1968. Chapter 2.

Woolf, Maurice D. and Jeanne A. Woolf. *Remedial Reading: Teaching and Treatment.* New York: McGraw-Hill Book Company, 1957. Chapter 1.

Zintz, Miles V. *Corrective Reading.* Dubuque, Iowa: William C. Brown Company, Publishers, 1966. Chapter 7.

3

Useful Standardized and Informal Tests

This chapter discusses the standardized and informal tests which can be used in different ways in any reading improvement program. Three individual intelligence tests and their relation to a reading improvement program are presented. Two group intelligence tests are presented, and their limitations for use in a reading improvement program are described. Also illustrated are two reading readiness tests as well as tests to determine ability in visual perception and auditory discrimination. This chapter also presents two standardized survey and two diagnostic reading tests, and the reader is referred to Appendices III and IV for additional titles. Two oral reading tests and two projective techniques are described. The selection of the tests within each category are arbitrary, but they are to be highly recommended for any teacher.

The construction and administration of an individual reading inventory is described. Several criteria are included which help the teacher to determine if a child really is a disabled reader. The construction of a group reading inventory also is included.

Intelligence Tests

Intelligence tests are used in a reading improvement program to determine if a child has the intellectual potential for reading improvement. An individual intelligence test is much more valid than a group intelligence test since any group intelligence test tends to measure reading ability as well as intelligence. Then a disabled reader does not score well on a group intelligence test, and the teacher does not think that he has the intellectual potential which he really does.

However, even an individual intelligence test is not a perfect measure of a child's intellectual ability since the results can be influenced by many factors. The test results can depend on the child's interest in taking the test, how he feels physically the day of the test, and the rapport which the examiner is able to establish with him. Even an individual intelligence test can be in error by more than ten IQ points in each direction.

An individual intelligence test usually should be administered by an elementary-school psychologist or guidance counselor. However, any teacher of reading can learn to give either one of the most valid individual tests if she takes a graduate course in individual testing from a local university. In such a course the teacher will have to practice giving the test many times under qualified supervision.

Many reading specialists believe that the Weschler Intelligence Scale for Children (WISC), Psychological Corporation, 304 East 45th Street, New York 10017, is the most valid individual intelligence test for use in either a corrective or remedial reading program. The WISC gives a verbal intelligence quotient, a performance intelligence quotient, and a full-scale intelligence quotient. Since the verbal score is considered the most highly related to reading success, most disabled readers score more highly in the performance area. The disabled reader usually scores the lowest on the subtests of information, arithmetic, and digit span, with the subtest of digit span being the lowest score of all. The following are the subtests found on the WISC:

Information—Measures the background of information which the child has. The culturally disadvantaged child often scores poorly on this subtest.

Comprehension—Measures a child's common sense and ability to use good judgment.

Arithmetic—Measures a child's ability in the reasoning which is required for success in arithmetic.

Similarities—Measures a child's ability in abstracting, generalizing, and conceptualizing.

Vocabulary—Measures the mental process required in acquiring vocabulary, and a culturally disadvantaged child usually does not do well on this subtest due to a poor experiential background.

Digit Span—Measures auditory memory, attention span, and ability to concentrate.

Picture Completion—Measures visual perception and the ability to notice details carefully.

Picture Arrangement—Measures visual perception and a child's ability to put a series of events in chronological order.

Block Design—Measures visual perception, hand-eye coordination, and the ability to copy a design.

Object Assembly—Measures visual perception, hand-eye coordination, and the ability to analyze and synthesize.

Coding—Measures visual perception, hand-eye coordination, left-to-right progression, and the ability to copy a series of symbols.

In the past the Stanford-Binet Intelligence Scale was more commonly used in reading improvement programs than it is at present. It still is a valuable test for determining mental age which can provide a point of reference in comparing mental maturity with reading achievement. The Stanford-Binet Scale can be obtained from the Houghton-Mifflin Company, 110 Tremont Street, Boston, Massachusetts 02107, and its subtests are Information and Past Learning, Verbal Ability, Memory Perception, and Reasoning Ability.

Since the Stanford-Binet Scale mainly measures verbal ability, many reading specialists believe that the WISC probably is better to use with disabled readers since it also measures performance ability. If a teacher gives either of these individual intelligence tests herself, she can learn much about a disabled reader by watching how he acts while taking the test. She can notice his attention span, his perserverance, his tenseness, or his insecurity.

There is one other individual intelligence test available which can be very useful in a reading improvement program since it does not require any reading ability on the part of a child who is taking it. It also is very easy to administer and score, and the teacher does not need any special training to learn to give it. This test also correlates quite highly with the Stanford-Binet Intelligence Scale and is as follows:

The Peabody Picture Vocabulary Test, American Guidance Service, Incorporated, Publishers Building, Circle Pines, Minnesota 55014

This test can be given to children from two and a half years to eighteen years of age and takes about fifteen minutes to give. It is a picture vocabulary test using a series of 150 plates that become more difficult. Each plate contains four pictures.

Two of the more commonly used group intelligence tests are mentioned in this chapter, and the reader can refer to Appendix I for a list of additional group intelligence tests. The caution must again be made that group intelligence tests tend to underestimate the reading potential of a disabled reader and *cannot* be used as a very valid indicator of a disabled reader's probable ability to profit from a reading improvement program. Two commonly used group intelligence tests are as follows:

Lorge-Thorndike Intelligence Tests, Houghton-Mifflin Company, 110 Tremont Street, Boston, Massachusetts, 02107

The non-verbal test is designed for grades kindergarten through twelve, and the verbal test is designed for grades four through twelve. The tests take thirty to sixty minutes to administer. Generally, the tests measure intellectual potential using the subtests of verbal reasoning ability, vocabulary, verbal classification, sentence completion, arithmetic reasoning, and verbal analogy.

The SRA Primary Mental Abilities Test, Science Research Associates, Incorporated, 259 East Erie Street, Chicago, Illinois 60611

This test is designed for grades kindergarten through twelve and takes about sixty minutes to administer. No reading is required in the primary test. The subtests are verbal meaning, perceptual speed, spatial ability, reasoning, and number sense.

Tests Used to Predict Reading Achievement

There are a number of reading readiness tests available which are used to predict reading achievement in the primary grades. Most of these tests correlate about .60 to .65 with first-grade reading achievement, and they are not considered to be infallible indicators of reading success. The total scores are a more useful predictor than are individual subtest scores, and their predictive power is the least good at the lower end of the range, or with children who do poorly on the tests. A complete list of reading readiness tests is found in Appendix II, but the following are two of the more commonly used reading readiness tests:

Metropolitan Readiness Tests, Harcourt, Brace and World, Incorporated, 757 Third Avenue, New York 10017

This test is designed for use in the latter half of kindergarten or the first part of first grade and takes about sixty minutes to administer. It contains the subtests of word meaning, sentence meaning, information, matching, copying, and a supplementary subtest asking the child to "draw a man."

The Murphy-Durrell Reading Readiness Analysis, Harcourt, Brace and World, Incorporated, 757 Third Avenue, New York 10017

This test is designed for use during the latter half of kindergarten, or the first part of first grade, and takes sixty minutes to administer. It contains the subtests of identifying separate sounds, in words spoken by the examiner, identifying capital and lower-case letters that are named by the examiner, and learning rate in which a child tries to recognize some sight words one hour after the examiner has taught them.

A test is available for measuring a child's visual perception ability either in kindergarten or in the early primary grades. The test yields a perceptual quotient and indicates if a child needs to have special training in visual perception. This test can be used very well to supplement a reading readiness test to predict primary-grade reading achievement and is the following:

The Frostig Developmental Test of Visual Perception, Consulting Psychologists Press, Palo Alto, California 94306

This test is used with children four and a half through seven and consists of the subtests of visual motor coordination, constancy of form, figure-ground relationships, position in space, and spatial relationships.

There is also a test available which very effectively measures a child's auditory discrimination. This test can be used in late kindergarten or early first grade as a supplement to a reading readiness test or can be used during the diagnostic phase of any reading improvement program to test a child's auditory discrimination. This test is as follows:

The Wepman Test of Auditory Discrimination, Language Research Associates, 950 East 59th Street, Chicago, Illinois 60650

For this test the examiner asks the child to sit with his back to her. The examiner then pronounces two words such as "tug" and "tub" or "lack" and "lack." The child is to tell the examiner if she has pronounced the two same words or two different words.

Standardized Survey Reading Tests

A standardized survey reading test is designed to gain a measure of a student's general or overall reading ability. A survey test is always a group test and is mainly designed to test paragraph comprehension and vocabulary knowledge. A few standardized survey reading tests also measure sentence comprehension and rate of reading. They usually are given to all children in an elementary-school classroom to determine each child's instructional reading level and the average reading level of all the students in the classroom. Each student who does poorly on a survey reading test should usually be given a standardized diagnostic reading test to determine his exact reading difficulties as well as some probable causes for these difficulties. Since a standardized survey reading test often overestimates a child's actual instructional reading level by one or two grades, it should be supplemented by using an individual reading inventory as described later in this chapter.

Primary-Grade Survey Tests

California Reading Tests, California Test Bureau, Del Monte Research Park, Monterey, California 93940

This test contains one battery for grades one and two and another battery for grades three through four and a half. It tests vocabulary knowledge and paragraph comprehension.

Gates-MacGinitie Primary Reading Test, Teachers College Press, Columbia University, New York 10027

This test is designed for grades one through three, and it tests vocabulary knowledge and paragraph comprehension with a supplementary test to measure reading rate.

Intermediate-Grade Survey Tests

Gates-MacGinitie Survey Reading Tests, Teachers College Press, Columbia University, New York, 10027

There is one test for grades four through six and another test for grades seven through nine. They measure vocabulary knowledge, general comprehension, and rate of reading.

Iowa Every-Pupil Tests of Basic Skills–Reading Comprehension and Work-Study Skills, Houghton-Mifflin Company, 110 Tremont Street, Boston, Massachusetts 02107

This test measures vocabulary, reading, spelling, and is unique in that it also measures the work-study skills of capitalization, punctuation, and usage, map reading, interpretation of graphs and tables, and use of reference materials.

There also are several achievement tests which can be used as survey reading tests. When they are used in this way, usually only the subtests of vocabulary (word meaning) and paragraph comprehension are used. There are different batteries for each of these two tests for use in the primary and intermediate grades. These tests are the following:

Metropolitan Achievement Test: Reading, Harcourt, Brace and World, Incorporated, 757 Third Avenue, New York 10017

This test has one battery for the last half of first grade, another battery for grade two, an elementary battery for grades three and four, and an intermediate battery for grades five to six. The two primary tests measure word knowledge and word discrimination, the elementary test adds reading comprehension, and the intermediate test measures word knowledge and reading comprehension.

Stanford Achievement Test: Reading, Harcourt, Brace and World, Incorporated, 757 Third Avenue, New York 10017

This test has a primary battery for grades one and two and an elementary battery for grades three and four. It also has an intermediate battery for grades five and six. It measures word meaning and paragraph comprehension.

Additional standardized survey reading tests are found in Appendix III.

Standardized Diagnostic Reading Tests

A diagnostic reading test attempts to determine a child's *exact* difficulties in reading. From a diagnostic reading test, a teacher can determine if a child's reading disability is due mainly to difficulties in phonetic analysis, word form clues, structural analysis, lower-type comprehension, or higher-type comprehension. Usually a diagnostic reading test is given individually to a disabled reader, but there are several diagnostic reading tests available which can be given on a group basis.

Diagnostic reading tests really do not attempt to determine the exact causes for a child's reading disability, but a teacher can often gain clues to the causes by carefully observing the child while he is taking a diagnostic reading test. The checklist found in the *Durrell Analysis of Reading Difficulty* (Figure 3-1) can be of great help in determining both reading difficulties and their causes.[1] It is the best checklist available at the present time according to many reading specialists.

Individual Diagnostic Reading Tests

Durrell Analysis of Reading Difficulty, Harcourt, Brace and World, Incorporated, 757 Third Avenue, New York 10017

This test is designed for grades one through six and takes about thirty to forty-five minutes to administer. It is made up of the subtests of oral reading, silent reading, listening comprehension, word recognition and word analysis, naming letters, identifying letter names, matching letters, writing letters, visual memory of words, hearing sounds in words, learning to hear sounds in words, learning rate, phonic spelling of words, spelling test, and handwriting test.

Spache Diagnostic Reading Scales, California Test Bureau, Del Monte Research Park, Monterey, California 93940

This test is designed for grades one through eight and has no time limit. It also can be used with disabled readers at the secondary school level. It contains three word recognition lists, twenty-two reading passages, and six supplementary phonics tests. It gives an instructional level in oral reading, an independent level in silent reading, and a potential level in auditory discrimination.

Group Diagnostic Reading Tests

Bond-Clymer-Hoyt Development Reading Test, Lyons and Carnahan Company, 407 East 25th Street, Chicago, Illinois 60616

This test is designed for use in grades three through eight and takes about forty-five minutes to administer in two sessions. It mainly is a silent reading test made up of the subtests of word recognition in isolation, recognition of words in context, recognition of reversible words in context, location of parts of words useful in word recognition, syllabication, locating root words, phonetic knowledge—general word elements, recognition of beginning sounds, selecting rhyming words, identification of letter sounds, and the ability to blend visually and phonetically.

Doren Diagnostic Reading Test Educational Test Bureau, 720 Washington Avenue, SE, Minneapolis, Minnesota 55014

This test is designed for grades from one through nine and is an untimed test. It tests knowledge in beginning sounds, sight words,

[1] Donald D. Durrell, *Durrell Analysis of Reading Difficulties,* (New York: Harcourt, Brace and World, Incorporated, 1955), p. 2.

Check List of Instructional Needs

NON-READER OR PREPRIMER LEVEL

Needs help in:

1. Listening comprehension and speech
___ Understanding of material heard
___ Speech and spoken vocabulary

2. Visual perception of word elements
___ Visual memory of words
___ Giving names of letters
___ Identifying letters named
___ Matching letters
___ Copying letters

3. Auditory perception of word elements
___ Initial or final blends
___ Initial or final single sounds
___ Learning sounds taught

4. Phonic abilities
___ Solving words
___ Sounding words
___ Sounds of blends — phonograms
___ Sounds of individual letters

5. Learning rate
___ Remembering words taught
___ Use of context clues

6. Reading interest and effort
___ Attention and persistence
___ Self-directed work

7. Other
___ ______
___ ______
___ ______
___ ______
___ ______

PRIMARY GRADE READING LEVEL

Needs help in:

1. Listening comprehension and speech
___ Understanding of material heard
___ Speech and spoken vocabulary

2. Word analysis abilities
___ Visual memory of words
___ Auditory analysis of words
___ Solving words by sounding
___ Sounds of blends, phonograms
___ Use of context clues
___ Remembering new words taught

3. Oral reading abilities
___ Oral reading practice
___ Comprehension in oral reading
___ Phrasing (Eye-voice span)
___ Errors on easy words
___ Addition or omission of words
___ Repetition of words or phrases
___ Ignoring punctuation
___ Ignoring word errors
___ Attack on unfamiliar words
___ Expression in reading
___ Speech, voice, enunciation
___ Security in oral reading
___ ______
___ ______
___ ______

4. Silent reading and recall
___ Level of silent reading
___ Comprehension in silent reading
___ Attention and persistence
___ Unaided oral recall
___ Recall on questions
___ Speed of silent reading
___ Phrasing (Eye movements)
___ Lip movements and whispering
___ Head movements Frowning
___ Imagery in silent reading
___ Position of book Posture
___ ______
___ ______
___ ______

5. Reading interest and effort
___ Attention and persistence
___ Voluntary reading
___ Self-directed work Workbooks

INTERMEDIATE GRADE READING LEVEL

Needs help in:

1. Listening comprehension and speech
___ Understanding of material heard
___ Speech and oral expression

2. Word analysis abilities and spelling
___ Visual analysis of words
___ Auditory analysis of words
___ Solving words by sounding syllables
___ Sounding syllables, word parts
___ Meaning from context
___ Attack on unfamiliar words
___ Spelling ability
___ Accuracy of copy Speed of writing
___ Dictionary skills: Location, pronunciation, meaning
___ ______
___ ______

3. Oral reading abilities
___ Oral reading practice
___ Comprehension in oral reading
___ Phrasing (Eye-voice span)
___ Expression in reading Speech skills
___ Speed of oral reading
___ Security in oral reading
___ Word and phrase meaning
___ ______
___ ______

4. Silent reading and recall
___ Level of silent reading
___ Comprehension in silent reading
___ Unaided oral recall
___ Unaided written recall
___ Recall on questions
___ Attention and persistence
___ Word and phrase meaning difficulties
___ Sentence complexity difficulties
___ Imagery in silent reading
___ ______

5. Speeded reading abilities
___ Speed of reading (Eye movements)
___ Speed of work in content subjects
___ Skimming and locating information

6. Study abilities
___ Reading details, directions, arithmetic
___ Organization and subordination of ideas
___ Elaborative thinking in reading
___ Critical reading
___ Use of table of contents References

7. Reading interest and effort
___ Voluntary reading
___ Variety of reading
___ Self-directed work

FIGURE 3-1

rhyming, whole word recognition, speech consonants, blending vowels, ending sounds, discriminate guessing, and letter recognition.

A listing of additional individual and group standardized diagnostic reading tests is found in Appendix IV.

Oral Reading Tests

An oral reading test is an individual test commonly given to disabled readers to determine their instructional grade level as well as to note common characteristics of oral reading such as word-by-word reading, finger pointing, or guessing words without using context clues. Each test contains a graded series of paragraphs which the child reads orally while the examiner marks his reading errors according to a prescribed plan. At the end of each oral reading paragraph, the examiner asks a few comprehension questions, and these usually are literal questions. The examiner also can check certain characteristics of the child's oral reading on his test blank. The following are two commonly used oral reading tests:

Gilmore Oral Reading Test, Harcourt, Brace and World, Incorporated, 757 Third Avenue, New York 10017

This test can be used in grades one through eight and takes about fifteen minutes to administer. It consists of ten oral reading paragraphs and measures comprehension, and speed and accuracy of comprehension.

Gray Oral Reading Test, Bobbs-Merrill Company, 4300 West 62nd Street, Indianapolis, Indiana

This test can be used in grades one through twelve and takes about fifteen minutes to administer. It is printed in four forms and has thirteen graded oral reading paragraphs. It is designed to measure oral reading ability and help in diagnosing reading difficulties.

A listing of several additional oral reading tests is found in Appendix V.

Projective Techniques

As was indicated in Chapter 3, sometimes a projective technique can effectively be used to determine some of the causes for reading difficulties. A projective technique enables an examiner to find out something about a child without the child's knowledge of what he is doing. Several projective techniques can be given by any teacher while a number of them must be administered by an especially trained person such as a psychologist or a guidance counselor. A teacher should not try to evaluate a projective technique that is designed to be evaluated by an especially trained professional person.

The first of the following two projective techniques can be given by the teacher, but it must be evaluated by a psychologist. The second projective technique can be both given and evaluated by a teacher, and using it she often can gain valuable clues as to how a disabled reader feels about himself, his family, and reading.

Goodenough Draw-a-Man Test. This test can be found in the book *Mental Testing.* New York: Holt, Rinehart and Winston, Incorporated, 1949

In this test the child is asked to draw the very best man he can on a blank sheet of paper using a pencil. This test does not measure artistic ability, but rather measures perception of detail, and how a child views himself. The test can be evaluated both in terms of the child's mental age and emotional adjustment. The teacher can judge the child's mental age, but a qualified person must judge his emotional adjustment.

Incomplete Sentences Test. The following Incomplete Sentences Test was written especially for disabled readers by Strang and others:

1. Today I feel*____________________
2. When I have to read, I____________________
3. I get angry when____________________
4. To be grown up____________________
5. My idea of a good time____________________
6. I wish my parents knew____________________
7. School is____________________
8. I can't understand why____________________
9. I feel bad when____________________
10. I wish teachers____________________
11. I wish my mother____________________
12. Going to college____________________
13. To me, books____________________
14. People think I____________________

---

*From *Diagnostic Teaching of Reading* by Ruth Strang. Copyright 1964, 1969 by McGraw-Hill, Inc. All rights reserved. Used with permission of McGraw-Hill Book Company.

15. I like to read about____________________
16. On weekends I____________________
17. I don't know how____________________
18. To me, homework____________________
19. I hope I'll never____________________
20. I wish people wouldn't____________________
21. When I finish school____________________
22. I'm afraid____________________
23. Comic books____________________
24. When I take my report card home____________________
25. I am at my best when____________________
26. Most brothers and sisters____________________
27. I'd rather read than____________________
28. When I read math____________________
29. The future looks____________________
30. I feel proud when____________________
31. I wish my father____________________
32. I like to read when____________________
33. I would like to be____________________
34. For me, studying____________________
35. I often worry about____________________
36. I wish I could____________________
37. Reading science____________________
38. I look forward to____________________
39. I wish someone would help me____________________
40. I'd read more if____________________
41. Special help in reading____________________
42. Every single word is____________________
43. My eyes____________________
44. The last book I read____________________
45. My mother helps____________________
46. Reading in school____________________
47. My father thinks reading____________________
48. I read better than____________________
49. My father helps____________________
50. I would like to read better than____________________

The teacher can modify this Incomplete Sentences Test in any way that she wishes depending on the age of the child that she wishes to give it to. Some of the items in this illustrative test may be too mature for a child in the elementary school. The teacher can gain much insight into a child's attitude toward reading by evaluating the responses on this test. As an example, items 2, 13,

15, 27, 32, 37, 41, 44, 46, and 50 are directly related to the child's attitude toward reading.[2]

The Individual Reading Inventory

An individual reading inventory certainly is the most useful technique which any classroom teacher or special reading teacher can use. It was described by Emmett Betts in 1957 and has been very widely used since then especially in reading clinics.[3] The individual reading inventory is used to determine a child's different reading levels and specific reading needs. It is used to determine a child's independent or free reading level (the level at which he can do easy recreational reading); the instructional reading level (the level at which he can receive actual reading instruction); the frustration reading level (the level at which reading is too difficult for him); and the potential or capacity level (the level at which he can answer comprehension questions effectively).

Betts has developed a classification scheme for determining these reading levels based on the child's performance on the graded oral reading paragraphs of the individual reading inventory. The independent or free reading level is the point at which the child can identify words with 99% accuracy and has 95% or better comprehension. The instructional reading level is the point at which a child can identify words with 90% accuracy and has 75% or better comprehension. The frustration level is the point at which a child is less than 90% accurate in word recognition and has less than 50% accuracy in comprehension. At the frustration level, a child also may show symptoms of withdrawal such as finger pointing, vocalizing, or wiggling in his chair. The potential or probable capacity level is the point to which the child can answer comprehension question after hearing a paragraph read aloud to him by the teacher. He can probably improve his reading ability to this level with proper corrective or remedial reading instruction.[4]

---

[2]Ruth Strang, *Diagnostic Teaching of Reading,* (New York: McGraw-Hill Book Company, 1969), pp. 262-263.

[3]Emmett A. Betts, *Foundations of Reading Instruction.* (New York: American Book Company, 1957).

[4]*Ibid.*

An individual reading inventory also can pinpoint a child's specific reading needs such as weaknesses in sight words, phonetic analysis, structural analysis, or comprehension. The individual reading inventory provides a very accurate measure of a child's instructional reading level, and this level often is from one to two grade levels lower than the score from a standardized survey reading test. Survey reading tests tend to overestimate a child's instructional reading level and instead tend to reflect his frustration reading level.

An individual reading inventory can be given to any child in an elementary classroom but is more widely used with children who have reading difficulties. It certainly should be given early in any reading improvement program to every disabled reader. It can again be emphasized that an individual reading inventory is an *absolutely* essential part of any reading improvement program.

An Outline of the Individual Reading Inventory

An individual reading inventory should begin with a conversation with the child in which the teacher establishes rapport with him and puts him at ease. She can do this by asking him to tell her about his family, his special interests, the subjects he likes best in school, how he feels about reading, or any other area which the conversation leads to. This is even important when the classroom teacher gives the individual reading inventory to one of her students, but is especially important when she gives it to a child whom she does not already know well.

Next the teacher can ask the child to tell her a story about something which he likes to do or about an event which has happened to him recently. This is using the language-experience approach, and the teacher can write the story on a piece of paper using manuscript writing (printing) as the child dictates it. The child can then be asked to read the story back aloud to the teacher. Later the teacher can type the story for the child on either a primary typewriter or a regular typewriter and give it back to him at some later time to read it silently and orally as well as illustrate it. Using a language-experience story helps to establish rapport with the child as well as showing the teacher how effectively he can read about his own experiences in his own language patterns.

The Dolch Basic Sight Word Test can be given next. This is a test of the child's ability to pronounce by sight the 220 service words which make up seventy percent of the words found in any basal reader first reader and sixty-five percent of the words found in any basal reader second reader. The child should know most of these words by sight by the time he is in the third grade. The test can be obtained from the Garrard Press, Champaign, Illinois 61820. The following is the grade level which is obtained by using the results of this test:

Dolch Words Known	*Equivalent Reading Level*
0-75	Pre-Primer
76-120	Primer
121-170	First Reader
171-210	Second Reader or Above
About 210	Third Reader or Above[5]

The teacher next can give a simple phonics inventory which she has designed individually for the child depending upon his age and estimated instructional reading level. The following phonics inventory should serve only as a sample, but the teacher can read these words to children with an approximate second grade instructional reading level:

Tell me what letters these words begin with:

butter	surprise	duck
red	window	happen
candy	find	make

Tell me what letters these words end with:

dream	miss	look
playground	help	feel
good	then	puppet

Tell me what two letters (consonant blends or digraphs) these words begin with:

crack	church	ship
thin	grow	clean
stop	play	fly

Tell me what two letters (consonant blends or digraphs) these words end with:

wish	past	dust
duck	dusk	fresh
church	much	with

---

[5] Miles V. Zintz. *Corrective Reading.* (Dubuque, Iowa: William C. Brown, Publishers, 1966), pp. 45.

From the preceding sample, the teacher also can see how she could construct a structural analysis inventory or a context clue inventory individually fitted to the child's instructional reading level.

The next part of an individual reading inventory really is the most important and involves the use of graded oral reading paragraphs. The child begins by reading one of the paragraphs orally which the teacher believes is well below his instructional reading level. While the child is reading orally, the teacher marks his errors according to a planned procedure such as the following:

Omissions — Circle the entire word or letter sound — (father)

Insertions — Insert with a caret — ^bump

Underline and write in all mispronunciations — spring (sprung)

Draw a line through a substitution and write it in — ~~saw~~ was

Use a wavy line to indicate a repetition — what

Put a check mark above a hesitation of more than five seconds[6] — ✓ sunny

After the child has finished reading each paragraph, the teacher asks him several literal and several higher-type comprehension questions about it, and she writes in the child's exact responses. She also asks him the meaning of a term which was found in the paragraph to see if he can use context clues.

The child continues reading the graded oral reading paragraphs until he reaches his frustration level, the point at which he makes many reading errors, becomes tense, or shows evidences of withdrawal. Later the teacher can have the child read the appropriate paragraphs silently and again orally to see if the silent reading practice helps his oral reading of the paragraphs. The teacher also can read one or two of the paragraphs which he did not reach in his oral reading to him. She then can ask him questions about each of these paragraphs and record his exact answers. This establishes his potential or capacity level, the reading grade level to which he should be able to read with proper reading instruction.

In constructing the oral reading paragraphs of an individual reading inventory, the teacher can use a series of basal readers as a guide. She then takes one reader from each grade level and using

---

[6]Ruth Strang, *Diagnostic Teaching of Reading.* (New York: McGraw-Hill Book Company, 1964), p. 62.

the words found in that reader constructs a short story which will appeal to the interest of a fairly broad age range. Some older disabled readers do not respond very well to childish stories even if they are on their own reading level.

The teacher then types each of these graded oral reading paragraphs using a primary typewriter which she attaches with glue to a piece of cardboard or oaktag (Figure 3-2). These copies are for the child to read.

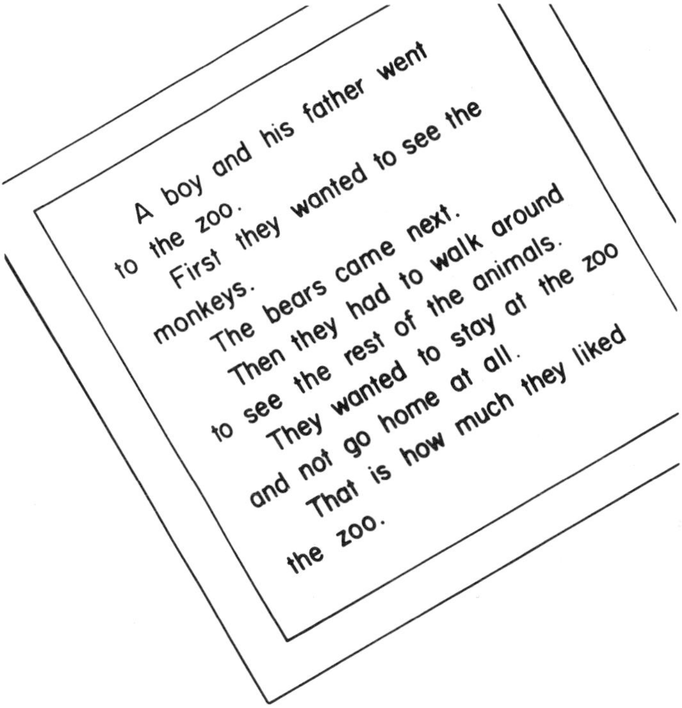

A boy and his father went
to the zoo.
First they wanted to see the
monkeys.
The bears came next.
Then they had to walk around
to see the rest of the animals.
They wanted to stay at the zoo
and not go home at all.
That is how much they liked
the zoo.

FIGURE 3-2

She types the paragraphs on separate sheets of paper double spaced with a regular typewriter, and she will mark the errors on these copies of the paragraphs. On each sheet of paper she also includes the comprehension questions she will ask as well as the manner in which she will determine the child's instructional and independent reading levels.

The teacher also can purchase individual reading inventories as found in the books: *Graded Selections for Informal Reading Diagnosis: Grades One Through Three, Graded Selections for*

Informal Reading Diagnosis: Grades Four through Six, and Classroom Reading Inventory.[7]

The following are the oral reading paragraphs for an individual reading inventory which have been constructed using the Harper and Row Basic Reading Program:[8]

A boy and his father went to the zoo.
First they wanted to see the monkeys.
The bears came next.
Then they had to walk around to see the rest of the animals.
They wanted to stay at the zoo and not go home at all.
That is how much they liked the zoo.

First Grade: A Trip to the Zoo

Questions:

1. Who went to the zoo?
2. What animal did they want to see first?
3. What would you like to see at the zoo?
4. What does the word "around" mean? Give me a sentence using the word "around."

Total number of words: 53		Accuracy:	
Number of words correct:		90%	48
		95%	50
Reading Time:	wpm	Comprehension Ability:	

Today was the first snow of the winter.
It was a very cold day.
In winter you can get your sled out of the garage.
Then you can have a good sled ride down your driveway.
When you are done, you can put your sled back into the garage.
Riding on your sled is just one way that you can have fun in winter.

Second Grade: Winter Fun

Questions:

1. Where can you put your sled when you aren't using it?
2. What is the weather usually like in winter?
3. Why should you put your sled back in the garage when you are done with it?

---

[7]Nila Banton Smith, *Graded Selections for Informal Reading Diagnosis: Grades One Through Three.* (New York: New York University Press, 1959); Nila Banton Smith, *Graded Selections for Informal Reading Diagnosis: Grades Four Through Six.* (New York: New York University Press, 1963); Nicholas J. Silvaroli, *Classroom Reading Inventory.* (Dubuque, Iowa: William C. Brown, Publishers, 1969).

[8]Mabel O'Donnell *et al., The Harper and Row Basic Reading Program.* (New York: Harper and Row, Publishers, 1966).

4. How else can you have fun in the winter?
5. What does the word "driveway" mean? Give me a sentence using the word "driveway."

Total number of words: 65	Accuracy:	
Number of words correct:	90%	59
	95%	62
Reading Time: wpm	Comprehension Ability:	

Timothy lived with his mother and father in a little white house in a quiet valley.
The streetcar did not go there, and the bus did not go that far.
Even the trains rolling all night in a bigger valley could not be heard.
Timothy loved his quiet valley.
Sometimes the valley was so quiet it made him wish that he could have a pet and a companion.
Someone to play with him in the valley.
He wanted to have a dog or cat.
Finally he got a duck for a pet.
It was a funny little whispering duck.

Third Grade: The Quiet Valley

Questions:

1. Where did Timothy live?
2. What did he want to have for a pet?
3. Why do you think the streetcar didn't go to his quiet valley?
4. Why do you think a duck is a good pet to have in the valley?
5. What is the word "companion?" Give me a sentence using the word "companion."

Total number of words: 100	Accuracy	
Number of words correct:	90%	90
	95%	95
Reading Time: wpm	Comprehension Ability:	

Homer Brown had played ball until it was almost dark, and now he was going home to his farm on the outskirts of town.
Homer took a short cut by the cemetery in the middle of some woods.
Many scary stories had been told by the boys at school about this area.
Something rattled.
Homer stopped in his tracks.
By the farthest tombstone in the very direction in which he was going, an indistinct white shape appeared to bob up and down.

For a moment, Homer stood frozen, unable to move.
When the thing came no closer, some of Homer's courage returned.
Trying to make no sound, he crept slowly past the other tombstones.
Once free of the woods he raced across the pasture, eyes straight ahead.

Fourth Grade: The Cemetery Ghost

Questions:

1. What had Homer done until it was almost dark?
2. What kind of sound did Homer hear?
3. Why do you think Homer couldn't move when he heard the sound?
4. Why do you think he passed the nearest tombstone very slowly and quietly?
5. What does the word "courage" mean? Give me a sentence using the word "courage."

Total number of words: 125	Accuracy:	
Number of words correct:	90%	113
	95%	119
Reading Time: wpm	Comprehension Ability:	

The dog had no name.
For a dog to have a name someone must have him and someone must love him, and a dog must have someone.
The dog had only the silent empty countryside of a few houses.
The dog had only the crumbs and clean bones he could pick up at a few houses.
He was a scared little whip-tailed cur.
He clung to a small area of the countryside just a few miles outside of town.
In a furtive, hidden, almost wild-animal way he had made it on his own.
The dog kept himself to the back fields, the wood lots, the fence rows, the shadows, and hedgerows.

Fifth Grade: The Cur

Questions:

1. Why did the dog have no name?
2. Where did he live?
3. Why do you think the dog became like a wild animal?
4. Why did he stay in the back fields away from people?
5. What do you think the word "furtive" means? Give me a sentence using the word "furtive."

Total number of words: 114 | Accuracy:
Number of words correct: | 90% 103
| 95% 108
Reading Time: wpm | Comprehension Ability:

A turtle lived in a pond at the foot of the hill.
Two young wild geese came to visit the turtle, and they became very well acquainted.
One day the geese said that they were going to a beautiful home far away, and that it would be a long and pleasant journey.
They told the turtle that he could go with them if he could keep his mouth shut and not say a word to anybody.
The turtle said he could do exactly as they wished.
So the next day the geese brought a stick, and they held the ends of it.
They told the turtle to take the middle of it in his mouth and not say a word until they reached home.
The geese then sprang into the air, with the turtle between them, holding fast to the stick.
Two village children saw the two geese flying along with the turtle and said: "Did you ever see anything more ridiculous in your life!"
The turtle looked down and began to talk.
When he let go, he fell dead at the feet of the children.

Sixth Grade: The Turtle Who Couldn't Stop Talking
Questions:

1. What did the geese say they were going to do?
2. What did the geese use to carry the turtle?
3. What did the two village children say?
4. What do you think the story is really trying to tell you?
5. Could this story really have happened?
6. What is the meaning of the word "ridiculous?" Give me a sentence using the word "ridiculous."

Total number of words: 193 | Accuracy:
Number of words correct: | 90% 174
| 95% 183
Reading Time: wpm | Comprehension Ability:

To conclude the individual reading inventory, the teacher can teach the child a few of the reading skills which he was found to be weak in. As an example, if the phonics inventory indicated that he was weak in the knowledge of short vowel sounds, the teacher can give him some concrete instruction in short vowel sounds. This helps the child to end the individual reading inventory with a feeling of success and the belief that he is going to make good progress in the reading improvement program.

Evaluating the Individual Reading Inventory

After the individual reading inventory is over, the teacher can evaluate the results. She can judge the child's ability in reading his own language patterns by observing how effectively he read the language-experience stories both during the inventory and several days later. She can evaluate his knowledge of sight words by the reading grade level established from giving him the Dolch Basic Sight Word Test. She can judge his knowledge of phonetic analysis, structural analysis, or use of context clues by evaluating the informal inventory given in each of these areas. She can evaluate his performance on the graded oral reading paragraphs by establishing his independent, instructional, frustration, and potential reading levels by using the classification scheme described earlier in this chapter.

All corrective or remedial reading instruction should begin slightly below or at the child's instructional reading level. All recreational reading which he does should be on his independent or free reading level.

Criteria for Determining Reading Disability

There are several criteria which can be used to determine if a child really is a disabled reader and can profit from either corrective or remedial reading instruction. The most common method in determining reading disability is the comparison of a child's score on an intelligence test and his score on a standardized survey reading and/or achievement test. The disabled reader often earns a higher score on the intelligence test than he does on the reading or achievement test, thus indicating that he has a good potential for reading improvement.

However, the caution has already been given that a group intelligence test tends to underestimate the intellectual ability of a disabled reader since it also tests reading ability. Therefore, the teacher may not see the potential for reading improvement which a disabled reader really has. A comparison between a child's score on an individual intelligence test and his score on a reading or achievement test gives the teacher a more valid indication of his potential for reading improvement.

A very valuable criterion for determining reading disability was designed by Guy Bond and Miles Tinker of the University of Minnesota. This criterion is called a reading expectancy formula and is as follows:[9]

Years in school x IQ + 1.0

Using this formula, the reader can see that a child with an intelligence quotient of 120 who is half way through the fourth grade would have a reading expectancy score of 5.2 (3.5 x 1.20 = 4.2 + 1.0 = 5.2).

Marion Monroe, formerly of the University of Chicago, also designed a criterion to determine reading disability. This measure uses the child's score on a standardized reading test and his score on a standardized arithmetic achievement test. If a child scores higher on the arithmetic test than he does on the reading test, Monroe concluded that he probably can make good reading progress in a reading improvement program.[10]

A listening comprehension test also can be used to determine if a child has the potential for good reading improvement. This chapter already has described how the graded oral reading paragraphs of the individual reading inventory can be used to determine a child's potential or probable capacity level. There also are several standardized listening comprehension tests. The child's score on the listening comprehension test is compared with his score on the standardized reading test to see if he can make good progress in a reading improvement program. Two of the more commonly used listening comprehension tests are as follows:

Brown-Carlsen Listening Comprehension Test, Harcourt, Brace and World, Incorporated, 757 Third Avenue, New York 10017

This test can be used in grades nine through thirteen and takes about fifty minutes to administer.

Durrell-Sullivan Reading Capacity Test, The Bureau of Educational

---

[9]Guy L. Bond and Miles A. Tinker, *Reading Difficulties: Their Diagnosis and Correction.* (New York: Appleton-Century-Crofts, 1967), p. 93.

[10]Marion Monroe, *Children Who Cannot Read.* (Chicago: University of Chicago Press, 1932).

Research and Service, Extension Division, University of Iowa, Iowa City, Iowa 52240

This test is designed to use in grades two through six. It takes about thirty minutes to administer. It uses pictures and has subtests of word meaning and paragraph meaning.

The Group Reading Inventory

Each intermediate-grade teacher needs to know how well the students in her class can read the textbooks designed for use in social studies and science. To find this out, she can design a group informal reading test to be used in each of these two content areas. This not only discovers if a child can read a textbook at its grade level designation, but also if he has the special reading skills needed for effective reading in these two areas.

To make an informal reading test either in social studies or science, the teacher chooses a section of about one thousand words from their textbook. This should be done just before the child is to read the textbook. After each child has read the selection, the teacher gives him some comprehension questions and vocabulary terms in a test which she has prepared. The comprehension questions should be of both the literal and higher-type. Critical and creative reading ability also can be tested. The teacher can also see in this informal test if a child has the specialized reading skills required for effective reading in these two subject areas. As an example, effective reading in social studies requires that a child have a good command of the specialized vocabulary, be able to interpret maps and graphs, be a critical reader, be able to see cause and effect relationships, and be able to apply what is read for problem-solving. To read effectively in science, a child must have a good command of the specialized vocabulary, be able to follow directions, be able to sense the sequence of events, and be able to apply what is read for problem-solving. The informal test also can include a test of vocabulary terms using a matching test or context clues.

An informal reading test can also judge a child's ability to use the entire textbook that he will read in social studies or science. This test also is given just before the children are to read the book. This test judges a child's ability to use the table of contents, the tables, the pictures, the subheads, and the glossary of the textbook.

If the reader wishes to see a sample of these informal reading tests, she can examine two books written by David Shepherd.[11]

SUMMARY

This chapter illustrated a number of standardized and informal tests that can be used in many ways in a reading improvement program. An individual intelligence test is much more valid to use in any reading improvement program since a group intelligence test tends to estimate reading ability as well as intellectual ability. The Weschler Intelligence Scale for Children and the Stanford-Binet Intelligence Scale and their part in a reading improvement program were discussed. Several group intelligence tests also were listed.

The value of reading readiness tests was discussed, and two of the most commonly used readiness tests were described. Two tests which can be used to supplement a reading readiness test were illustrated. They are the Frostig Developmental Test of Visual Perception and the Wepman Test of Auditory Discrimination.

A standardized survey reading test measures a child's general reading ability in the areas of vocabulary knowledge and paragraph comprehension. A survey test tends to overestimate a child's actual instructional reading level. Several survey reading tests were described in the chapter.

A standardized diagnostic reading test attempts to determine a child's exact reading difficulties and some probable causes for these difficulties. They usually are individual tests, but some of them can be given to a group of children. Four diagnostic reading tests were illustrated in this chapter.

An oral reading test is given individually to a child to determine his instructional grade level and common characteristics of oral reading. Two oral reading tests were described in this chapter.

A projective technique enables an examiner to learn different things about a child without the child's knowledge of what the examiner is trying to do. Most projective techniques must be given and evaluated by a psychologist or guidance counselor. The

---

[11]David Shepherd, *Effective Reading in the Social Studies.* (New York: Harper and Row, Publishers, 1961); David Shepherd, *Effective Reading in Science.* (New York: Harper and Row, Publishers, 1960).

Draw-a-Man Test was illustrated, and an Incomplete Sentences Test was included.

The individual inventory is a very useful technique for any teacher. It is used to determine a child's various reading levels and specific reading needs. The independent, instructional, frustration, and capacity levels, were described. An outline of an individual reading inventory was included in the chapter. It can include a preliminary conversation, a language-experience story, the Dolch Basic Sight Word Test, a phonics or structural analysis inventory, the graded oral reading paragraphs, and the teaching of a few of the reading skills that the child was found to be weak in. A sample of the graded oral reading paragraphs was included. Suggestions for evaluating the results of the individual reading inventory were included.

Several criteria for determining reading disability were described in this chapter. They were the comparison between an intelligence test score and a reading test score, the use of the reading expectancy formula, the comparison between a child's reading score and arithmetic score, and the use of a listening comprehension test. Descriptions of two listening comprehension tests were included.

A group reading inventory consists of informal reading tests in either social studies or science to see if a child can effectively read the textbook that he is going to later use. This inventory mainly is used in the intermediate grades or above.

REFERENCES

Carter, Homer L. J., and Dorothy J. McGinnis. *Diagnosis and Treatment of the Disabled Reader.* New York: The Macmillan Company, 1970. Chapters 7 and 8.

Dechant, Emerald. *Diagnosis and Remediation of Reading Disability.* West Nyack, New York: Parker Publishing Company, 1968. Chapter 2.

Strang, Ruth. *Diagnostic Teaching of Reading.* New York: McGraw-Hill Book Company, 1969. Chapters 7, 10, and 11.

Strang, Ruth. *Reading Diagnosis and Remediation.* Newark, Delaware: IRA Research Fund, 1968. Chapter 4.

Woolf, Maurice D. and Jeanne Woolf. *Remedial Reading: Teaching and Treatment.* New York: McGraw-Hill Book Company, Incorporated, 1957. Chapters 3 and 4.

4

Corrective and Remedial Reading Instruction

Thus far the reader has seen that reading difficulties usually are caused by several factors, and that it often is difficult to pinpoint one single cause of reading problems. Chapter 3 described a number of standardized survey and diagnostic reading tests which are useful in determining reading levels and specific reading weaknesses. Chapter 3 also illustrated the construction and administration of an individual reading inventory for determining reading levels and specific reading difficulties. Also illustrated was the use of several projective techniques for helping to determine the causes of reading disability.

This chapter explains corrective and remedial reading instruction, suggests several principles of reading remediation, and gives many practical suggestions for implementing a reading improvement program in the light of diagnosed reading difficulties. It also presents a sample teacher-disabled reader interview, and gives two illustrative case studies showing how a reading improvement program was actually conducted with two disabled readers.

Corrective and Remedial Reading Instruction

The reader should understand in which way the terms

corrective and remedial reading instruction are used in this book. They are used in the way that most of today's reading specialists use them.

Corrective reading instruction is given to a child or to a small group of children in the regular elementary classroom by the classroom teacher at some time during the school day. It is given to those children who are not severely disabled in reading and who do not show emotional disturbance about their reading. Such children usually have only a few reading difficulties which can be corrected by the classroom teacher when she uses a reading improvement program which was especially designed for them in the light of their diagnosed reading difficulties.

However, remedial reading instruction is provided by a special reading teacher in an elementary-school reading clinic, private reading clinic, or college reading clinic. Usually it is given to those children who are moderately or severely disabled in reading and who often have emotional problems caused by their lack of reading ability. Such children often have a number of reading difficulties which can be remediated in a program of reading improvement especially constructed for them in the light of their diagnosed reading deficiencies.

In either case, corrective or remedial reading instruction normally is good teaching of reading on a child's instructional reading level and specifically directed toward each child's diagnosed reading difficulties. It can employ any of the following methods and materials which also are used to teach developmental reading: basal readers, special phonics workbooks, the language-experience approach, individualized reading, a linguistic approach, the initial teaching alphabet, words in color, programmed workbooks, teacher-made worksheets, or phonics and reading games.

General Principles of Reading Improvement

There are several learning theories and principles of corrective and remedial reading instruction which should be carefully considered before a program of reading improvement is begun. They are as follows:

1. Corrective and remedial reading instruction is good developmental teaching of reading. Contrary to what is believed by many laymen, both corrective and remedial reading instruction really is developmental teaching of reading using several of the same approaches that are used in an elementary

classroom. Any developmental reading approach can be used in a program of reading improvement although normally a child should not be taught solely by an approach at which he has previously failed. Usually a combination of approaches or a method featuring the use of the child's preferred mode of learning may be used. In either case, the corrective or remedial reading instruction always is presented either on the child's instructional or independent reading level and is reinforced on the child's independent reading level.

2. Corrective or remedial reading instruction always is presented in the light of the child's diagnosed reading difficulties. This principle applies equally to developmental reading instruction, but must be very carefully considered in a program of reading improvement. For example, if a child's performance on a standardized diagnostic reading test has shown that he does not have mastery of the short vowel sounds, he should receive specific instruction in this area perhaps using pages from basal reader workbooks or special phonics workbooks to correct his difficulty.

3. Corrective or remedial reading instruction should always be based upon a child's present strengths. Any program of reading improvement must build upon a child's present reading strengths no matter how limited they may seem to be. Every child with a reading problem has some strengths which can be used as a starting point. These strengths can be discovered from examining the child's diagnostic reading test or his individual reading inventory. Each disabled reader must be made aware of his reading strengths since it is very important for him to know that he has some positive factors in his reading. For example, a child whose oral language ability is better than his reading ability may profit from the use of the language-experience approach early in a program of reading improvement since this approach effectively capitalizes on his oral language ability.

4. The general principles of human growth and development should be applied to a program of reading improvement. All of these principles are equally applicable to the developmental teaching of reading and to a program of reading improvement. Each disabled reader should be considered an individual in terms of his physical, intellectual, social, and emotional characteristics. The teacher's consideration of individual differences is important for every child, but is of extreme importance to a disabled reader. If a disabled reader's special needs are not considered, he probably will not have as much success as he could in a program of reading improvement.

5. A corrective or remedial reading program needs to show the child that he is making real improvement in reading. He needs to be convinced of this in a concrete way. Such tangible proof of his reading progress may be a chart showing progress in the areas in which he is receiving help, a list of the books he has read, or the construction of some objects that are made as the result of the reading improvement program. It is true that in working with disabled readers: "Nothing succeeds like observed success."

6. The teacher-pupil relationship is vital to the success of a reading

improvement program. The teacher's genuine feelings of concern and acceptance that she has for a disabled reader may be crucial to the success that he may have in the reading improvement program. Possibly the teacher-pupil relationship is the most important factor that influences the success of a reading improvement program.

7. The corrective or remedial program must be a structured program using the diagnosed difficulties. Therefore, before beginning a program of reading improvement, the teacher must outline the program. However, the program must be flexible enough to allow it to be changed in the light of later diagnosis. Since diagnosis and remediation of reading difficulties should go hand in hand, the formal and informal diagnoses which occur during the program should somewhat change the program of reading improvement. However, any program of reading improvement should contain direct and structured teaching.

8. If a child is found to have a number of areas of difficulties in his reading, the reading improvement program should begin with teaching the reading skills that are the most basic. For example, if a child has been found to have an instructional reading level at the latter first-grade level, word recognition skills probably should receive more emphasis than does higher-type comprehension. Obviously, a child cannot make conclusions or generalizations about his reading if he cannot identify the words found in the reading materials.

9. The teacher should get the disabled reader's help in understanding his reading problem and planning the reading improvement program. Many intermediate-grade children can help the teacher to understand their reading problem and its causes if the teacher asks them for their help. It is also helpful for a disabled reader to have a part in planning his program of reading improvement and to have some concrete role in implementing the reading improvement program.

10. The corrective or remedial reading period should not become too long or boring for the disabled reader. A half hour to one hour period is long enough for most children. If the session lasts half an hour, the teacher should plan for at least two different kinds of activities. If the session lasts for about one hour, the teacher should plan three to four different kinds of activities. This does not indicate that a child should move from one activity to another without finishing them. However, it is very important that a disabled reader not get bored with any one kind of activity. The child also should be actively involved in learning to read at all times.

Illustrations of How Remediation Is Based Specifically on Diagnosis

One of the most important principles of either corrective or remedial reading instruction is that it should be based specifically on diagnosed reading difficulties. The specific approach differs from a "shotgun" approach in which a disabled reader is presented with a wide variety of corrective instruction, some of which he does not need to have.

The specific deficiencies that a disabled reader has can be determined from a standardized diagnostic reading test such as the Durrell Analysis of Reading Difficulty, the Spache Diagnostic Reading Scales, the Developmental Reading Test, or the Doren Diagnostic Reading Test as were described in Chapter 3. The checklist of the Durrell Analysis of Reading Difficulty may also give insight into the specific reading needs that a disabled reader may have. The individual reading inventory also may point up specific reading difficulties.

If a disabled reader is found to lack mastery of the 220 basic sight words that are found on the Dolch Basic Sight Word Test that usually is given in the individual reading inventory, he should be given specific instruction in the learning of the service words by the use of word form clues (the use of the total word shape or configuration). These service words can be taught using flash cards with one of the words printed on each card or by a game devised by Dolch and published by the Garrard Publishing Company.[1] It is essential that each child *thoroughly* master these 220 service words as they are of first importance of reading improvement.

A disabled reader's weaknesses in phonetic analysis usually can be exactly determined to the extent that he may be found to need instruction in the short vowel sounds. When his needs and phonetic analysis are determined, the teacher can begin instruction using appropriate pages from a basal reader workbook, teaching the extending skills and abilities part of an appropriate basal reader lesson, using appropriate pages from a special phonics workbook, using teacher-made phonetic worksheets, or employing commercially prepared or teacher-prepared games which teach or review the short vowel sounds.

Instruction in the word recognition technique or structural analysis should also be specific to the extent that it may stress the teaching of syllabication and the blending of syllables if a disabled reader is weak in this area. To teach the skills of structural analysis, the teacher may use the appropriate basal reader work-

[1]E.W. Dolch, Basic Sight Vocabulary Cards (Champaign, Illinois: Garrard Press).

book pages, teach the extending skills and abilities part of an appropriate reader lesson, use teacher-made worksheets, employ commercially prepared or teacher-made word wheels, (Figure 4-1), or use commercially prepared or teacher-made games.

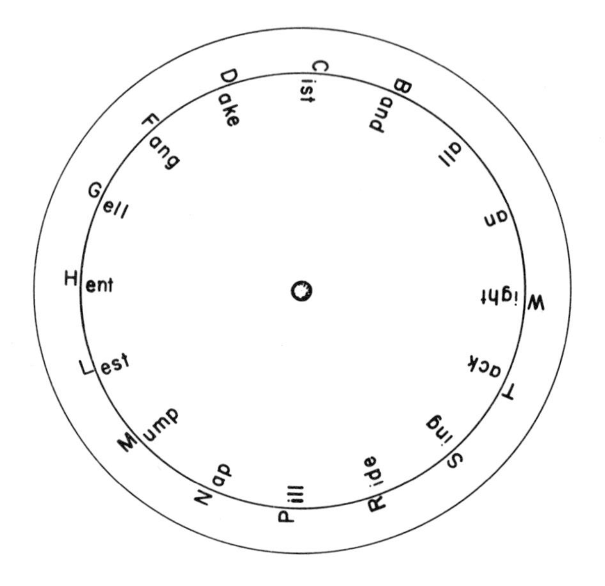

FIGURE 4-1

A disabled reader may be found to be weak in the use of context or meaning clues, and this difficulty may be most easily diagnosed by the teacher's listening to the child while he is reading the oral reading paragraphs of the individual reading inventory. While they are reading these paragraphs orally, sometimes the disabled readers do not supply unknown words that make sense in the sentences. Materials that were devised by McKee and Harrison can be useful in correcting this difficulty since these materials effectively use context clues and the initial consonant sounds in the following way:

Mary went for a ride on a tr__________.

tray
train
tree[2]

---

[2]Paul McKee, Anne McCowen, Lucile Harrison, Elizabeth Lehr, and William Durr, *The Reading for Meaning Series* (Boston: Houghton Mifflin Company, 1966).

The teacher also may use the basal reader workbook pages on the child's instructional reading level that teach the use of context clues. The teacher also can construct worksheets to teach the use of context clues in the following form:

The little boy would like to fly in an ________.

around
airplane
about

Disabled readers in the elementary school usually need to have the value and use of context clues explained to them in detail if they are to be able to use them. Probably some children who do not use context clues think that this is just guessing at an unknown word and not a "correct" way to get the meaning.

Most elementary-school disabled readers have difficulty with word recognition and many less have difficulty with comprehension. However, there are children in the elementary school that have good word recognition techniques but are diagnosed as having difficulty with comprehension by the use of a standardized diagnostic test or by the use of the comprehension questions following the oral reading paragraphs of an individual reading inventory. For this reason the comprehension questions used in an individual reading inventory should test both literal and higher-type comprehension as sometimes children have good literal comprehension ability but cannot answer inferential comprehension questions.

The teacher can use a variety of techniques to correct difficulty with comprehension. One valuable way is to group a few disabled readers who have a similar instructional reading level and similar comprehension difficulties. Then the directed reading activity which involves using a basal reader story and the comprehension questions found in the teacher's manual can be used. The manual gives both literal and higher-type comprehension questions, and the teacher can emphasize the kind of comprehension that the group of children have the most difficulty with.

In additon, to improve reading comprehension the teacher can make up her own comprehension questions for any basal reader story. The workbooks of the basal readers also contain pages with both literal and higher-type comprehension questions. A disabled reader can read tradebooks on his instructional reading level and the teacher can ask him literal and higher-type comprehension questions about a tradebook during the individual reading conference. Directions which ask children to do something or make something after reading them can be used with a disabled reader who is especially weak in comprehension—those children who can accurately pronounce words but cannot understand what they are reading (word callers). Directions often can be typed on a strip of paper or oaktag and tell the children what to do. For example:

> Go to the door and open it. Then come back and sit in your chair.
>
> Look in the upper right-hand drawer of my desk. You may keep what you find in it.
>
> Draw a picture of your house on a piece of paper. You can also draw each person in your family standing in front of the house.

The Teacher's Role in Reading Improvement

The teacher-pupil relationship is of the *utmost* importance in determining whether a disabled reader will make good progress in a program of either corrective or remedial reading instruction. The teacher must be able to accept each disabled reader with his difficulties and be able to help him develop a positive self-concept. The disabled reader often has been rejected by his parents even before school entrance since he could not live up to their expectations for him even then. He usually has met defeat in all learning experiences in school. The disabled reader then has often become emotionally involved with his reading disability to the point that he feels negatively toward all reading situations usually including any teacher that tries to help him improve his reading.

Sometimes it takes quite a while for a teacher to gain a disabled reader's confidence. Also the teacher must not underestimate the child's potential reading ability nor underestimate how a child with a reading problem feels about it. If a disabled reader acts as though reading is not important to him, the teacher should remember that he may not want to admit how important reading is to him. The teacher should never become so emotionally involved with a disabled reader that she cannot be objective in helping him.

It is also very important for the teacher to give a disabled reader reading tasks with which he always can experience success.

He usually will not make progress in reading if the tasks he has to do are too difficult for him. However, his reading tasks should not appear "babyish" to him, but should be difficult enought to give him a challenge. The disabled reader needs to see his reading progress in some concrete way such as using progress charts, gold stars, or another form of extrinsic motivation. The teacher should also praise a disabled reader for what he has accomplished, but her praise must be given only when he really has accomplished something.

The importance of the teacher-pupil relationship in a program of reading improvement cannot be overemphasized. It is difficult to describe the relationship, but the teacher must be warm, permissive, well-organized, and able to demand as much progress of a disabled reader as his capabilities let him make.

The Individual or Group Reading Conference

If children are to be grouped for either corrective or remedial reading instruction, they should be grouped on the basis of a similar instructional reading level and diagnosed reading needs. However, more often the corrective or remedial reading instruction is given on an individual basis.

Since corrective reading instruction is given by the classroom teacher, she may know much about a disabled reader's reading needs and interests. If this is the case, she may begin corrective reading instruction by giving an individual reading inventory if the child has not already had one.

The reading teacher usually does not know the disabled reader with whom she is to work in remedial reading instruction and has to establish rapport with him at the first meeting. The main objective of the first meeting is to establish a friendly and warm relationship with the disabled reader and there are several ways of doing this. The teacher can give an individual reading inventory if she includes finding out about the disabled reader's background and interests at this time. The teacher also can use the child's interests by finding out about them from his classroom teacher and having something at the first meeting that will interest him. For example, if the teacher discovers that a child is interested in making model airplanes, she may bring a model airplane kit with typed directions which she thinks he can read and follow to make the model during the first meeting.

A number of reading specialists feel that the first few meetings in either corrective or remedial reading instruction should be devoted to the diagnosis of specific reading difficulties by the use of either a standardized diagnostic reading test or an individual reading inventory. Such a diagnosis then can point the way to later correction without teaching the child some reading skills that he already knows. They also believe that diagnosis should be continuous with the teacher diagnosing reading difficulties every time she works with a child either in a group or individual setting.

However, other reading specialists feel that the diagnosis and correction of reading difficulties should always be interwoven even from the first meeting. This makes sure that a disabled reader does not become emotionally blocked from the difficulty he may have with the tests that are given to him at the first several meetings. Such reading specialists think that most disabled readers have performed poorly on reading tests in the past and are therefore negative toward the whole procedure. Such reading specialists further believe that each disabled reader should receive concrete help from the first meeting. This book emphasizes continuous or interwoven diagnosis and remediation whether the disabled reader is in a classroom or reading clinic.

In either case, the first meeting for reading improvement should point the way toward later corrective or remedial reading instruction. A disabled reader's view of his own reading strengths and weaknesses can also be discovered during the first meeting. Many intermediate-grade children are very knowledgeable about their own reading difficulties and its causes. The teacher and child can then together work to plan the reading improvement program as it progresses. A disabled reader who is actively involved in planning his own reading improvement program usually puts forth more effort.

Some of the characteristics of a good initial interview can be seen in the following interview which took place between Mrs. Edwards, an elementary-school special reading teacher, and Jim, a twelve-year-old disabled reader who had been referred for remedial reading instruction by his classroom teacher. At the time of this initial interview, Jim was in the early part of sixth grade and his instructional reading level was approximately on the early third-grade reading level. He had repeated second grade and still had negative feelings toward all reading activities.

Initial Interview with Jim

Teacher: Are you Jim?

Jim: Yeah, my name is Jim, and I am supposed to get help with my reading from you. I really didn't want to come, but my teacher said that I had to.

T: I hope I can help you with your reading, and I know that I will try to make our work together just as interesting as I possibly can. Before you sit down, could you close the door for me.

J: O. K. (Jim sits down in a chair directly across the table from the teacher.)

T: Can you tell something about your reading problem? Why don't you like to read and what is there about reading that gives you the most trouble?

J: I don't know, but I just can't seem to get the words that I don't already know. When I come to a word I don't know, I usually skip it cause that's the easiest for me. I just hate reading anyway since it just isn't that important. Anyway my folks don't think reading good is important either.

T: You probably have the most trouble with sounding out the words you don't know or breaking them apart into syllables. Can you use a dictionary?

J: Naw, I don't know how to use a dictionary. I guess my teachers never had time to show me.

T: Do you think that you can understand what you are reading?

J: Yah, pretty well except if there are too many words that I don't know, then I have trouble.

T: Do you remember how long you have had trouble with reading?

J: I really don't remember for sure, but probably since second grade. I flunked second grade, you know.

T: Now can you tell me a little about your family. What does your father do for a living, and do you have any brothers and sisters?

J: My father works in a factory–I really don't know what he does there. I have two brothers and two sisters. They're all older than me. My mother works now as a waitress in a restaurant.

T: You told me before that your mother and father don't think that reading is important?

J: Sure, they say that they both got along fine without reading very good. But both my older sisters did read pretty well in school. Both my brothers had trouble like me.

T: Could you tell me something about what you like to do best of all? (At this point the teacher may want to give orally all or part of the individual reading inventory which is found in this chapter.)

J: Mostly I like all sports. I guess I like to play baseball best of all. I am real good in sports, you know.

T: Isn't that wonderful! You know that's something that I'm not good in at all. I guess that we are all good in something. I am pretty sure that with your help I am going to be able to help you read much better. I have a book on baseball right here that we will look at together for a few minutes. (The teacher can choose a book on baseball from her library which is a high interest low-vocabulary trade book on the late second-grade reading level.)

The teacher and Jim spend about the next ten minutes looking at the book together. The teacher may want to read a little of the book at the beginning orally to Jim, and then the teacher and Jim can take turns reading a paragraph of the book orally if he is willing to do so. If Jim is motivated to read the book since it is interesting to him and since it is easy for him to read, he can take the book home with him to read before the next session.

At this point, the teacher may wish to give Jim the individual reading inventory which is found in Chapter 3 or an individual reading inventory which she has constructed for herself. From this inventory, the teacher will be able to determine exactly Jim's independent, instructional, frustration, and capacity levels. At the end of the inventory the teacher can teach Jim several skills which he has shown a need for, in this case probably some simple phonetic analysis skills. The interview can be concluded in this way:

Teacher: Well, you have certainly done very well today. Somehow I feel sure that together we are going to be able to help you make real reading improvement. Don't forget to take your book on baseball with you.

Jim: Thanks.

The reader can see from the first interview with Jim that the teacher tried to enlist Jim's help in finding out what his reading problem was. From his answers the teacher can assume that he has the most difficulty with the word recognition skills of phonetic analysis, structural analysis, and dictionary usage. She also can assume that his stock of sight words is satisfactory since his difficulty began in second grade when phonetic analysis began to receive emphasis. He probably would not have a great deal of difficulty with comprehension if he had a good method of attacking unknown words. Of course, all these tentative impressions would be either verified or disproven by the individual reading inventory which was given during the first interview.

Part of Jim's reading problem also may result from the indifference shown toward reading by his parents. This probably even influenced Jim's beginning experiences with reading. This interview also shows how Jim's interest in sports was used even in the beginning stages of reading improvement. It also indicates why it is important for him to read much material which is very easy for him to read so that he gets a successful experience with reading. Jim's cooperation and help also was enlisted in this first interview as it also should be in later interviews.

During the entire reading improvement program, each disabled reader's interests should be carefully considered. Interest does lead to increased effort, and using a child's interests either in a corrective or remedial reading program can make the difference between its success or failure. A disabled reader's interests can be discovered during the first several meetings by the teacher's talking with him in a friendly way or in the preliminary conversation that often starts an individual reading inventory. Interests also can be discovered through an interest inventory such as the following:

____
Name

1. After school I like to ____________________.
2. My hobby is ____________________.
3. When I grow up I want to ____________________.
4. I like to read stories about ____________________.
5. The favorite book I have ever read is ____________________.
6. More than anything else, I like to ____________________.
7. My favorite subject in school is ____________________.
8. On Saturday I like to ____________________.
9. My favorite toy is ____________________.
10. My favorite television program is ____________________.
11. My favorite game is ____________________.
12. I like to collect ____________________.
13. When I am home, I like to make ____________________.
14. I had the most fun ever when I ____________________.
15. If I could have anything in the world, I would like to have ________ ____________________________.

When a disabled reader's interests have been discovered, the teacher and child then can together find some ways to use the interests in the reading improvement program. Probably there are as many creative ways to use a child's interests in a reading improvement program as there are creative teachers and children. However, the following examples serve to illustrate how interests can be used in a reading improvement program.

Sometimes a disabled reader's interests can be used to help establish a good relationship with him. As an example, a boy in the later primary grades (a nonreader) came to a college reading clinic for help. He was emotionally blocked toward all reading activities and would not try to learn any reading skills. Therefore, his reading teacher used his interest which was building models for a whole semester and spent no time on reading instruction. Instead, his teacher just helped him build the models that he liked. However, by the end of the semester the teacher had established a good relationship with him, and the child had overcome his dislike of reading activities. The teacher then was able to begin remedial reading instruction at the preprimer stage, and the child made much reading improvement in a short time.

However, usually the disabled reader's interests and the reading improvement program can go hand in hand. For example, a child who is interested in building airplane models or model cars can have teacher-written directions to read and follow, and the teacher and child together can build the model after the child has read and understood the directions.

Any interests that a disabled reader has can be explored by him after the teacher has located materials about the interests from textbooks on the child's instructional reading level, trade-books, children's magazines and newspapers, or children's reference books.

At one college reading clinic a junior high school girl was interested in making a dress for herself, but she could not read the dress pattern directions effectively. The teacher and student together orally read the directions for making the dress, and the teacher wrote simplified directions which were dictated by the student. The student then took the simplified directions home and with the help of her mother made her dress carefully following the simplified directions.

Many interests can be explored by the disabled reader's taking trips to various places such as the grocery store, the farm, or the zoo. In each case, the child can be prepared in advance for what he may see by talking with his teacher about it. This kind of discussion will enable him to receive much more from the trip in terms of vocabulary and; concept development. The teacher and child then can take the trip together with the teacher's pointing out interesting things so that the child can get as much as possible from it in terms of vocabulary and concept development. After returning to the classroom or clinic, the child can dictate a language-experience story or write an experience story about the trip. This trip can also be illustrated by the child.

Teachers can prepare special materials for a disabled reader which will motivate him to read. One example is a teacher-written story about the child and something that she likes to do. An example of such a story is the following:

> Once there was a girl in second grade named Mary.
> Mary had a doll that she just loved.
> The name of Mary's doll was Susan.
> She played with Susan every day after school.
> Mary and Susan really were very good friends.

Another example are teacher-written directions which require the learner to read and do what they say. The teacher also can make up jokes and riddles for a disabled reader which involve him personally in some way.

The language-experience approach also can be used with photographs of a disabled reader and stories which he dictates about himself. The teacher can photograph the child doing certain things which interest him and later have him dictate or write experience stories about what he is doing in each photograph. Later the photographs and experience stories can be bound into an experience booklet for the child to read to his teacher and at home to his parents.

If a child has a special interest which can be used to suggest a certain reading method, his wishes can be considered in choosing the method. For example, if a child is especially interested in colors, words in color may be a good method (but not the only method) of teaching him how to read.

Two Illustrative Case Studies

The final reports of two actual case studies of disabled

readers are included so that the reader can see how all of the principles and practices of a reading improvement program are incorporated. They are included for the purpose of clarifying the concepts presented in this chapter and would, of course, have to be modified in the light of different factors for each disabled reader.

FIRST CASE SUMMARY

I. Identifying Data

A. Name: Jack Martin
B. Age: 10
C. Sex: Male
D. Grade: 5th
E. Ethnic Group: White
F. Teacher: Miss Betty Sampson

II. Brief Description of Client

The physical status of Jack seems good. He appears to be well built and well nourished. He is neat in appearance. His hearing tested normal and no visual difficulties were detected. Jack is of average intelligence. He has a friendly attitude and is very cooperative and anxious to learn during the work periods. He is interested in animals, adventure stories, and sports.

III. Problem

Jack's mother noticed that Jack skipped or misconstrued simple words in his reading. She feels that he guesses as he doesn't seem able to sound out words. She was surprised at his poor grades in the other subjects also.

The school records show that Jack needs help in reading as he isn't keeping up in his school subjects due to his poor reading ability. His teacher said that this is partly due to his short attention span, his daydreaming in school, and his annoying mannerisms to get attention in class.

IV. Family Composition

Jack comes from a large family. He is the youngest of seven children. There are six boys and one girl. His parents are divorced. Jack lives with his mother and brothers and sister. He sees his father on weekends. He also sees his grandmother on weekends, but he has missed out on attention from his grandparents that the other children received as his grandfather died and his grandmother is not in good health. Jack seems to feel that he is ignored in his family and would like to receive more attention. His brothers aren't too sympathetic toward him and expect too much of him in their sports activities at his age. His mother is trying to give more attention to Jack, but he needs more than she finds time to give him.

V. Contacts

The first meeting with Jack was September 20, 1967. The last interview was December 13, 1967. In all there was a total of thirteen meetings.

VI. Summary of Test Results

Previous tests show that Jack had been given the SRA Primary Mental Abilities Test on October 12, 1965 with an I.Q. of 107. The Weschler Intelligence Scale for Children (WISC) was given to Jack on September 27, 1967 and showed a verbal I.Q. of 94 and a performance I.Q. of 110. On October 2, 1967 he was given the California Test of Mental Maturity which indicated an I.Q. of 90.

Reading tests from grade 2 through 4 indicated that Jack needed help in reading, but each year he was promoted. In fourth grade, his classroom teacher tried to give him some special help.

Jack was given the Dolch Sight Word Test. He made nine errors which would indicate that he should begin to read on a third grade level.

The teacher then gave Jack an individual reading inventory using the Scott, Foresman readers. Although the Dolch Test indicated a reading level of third grade, the teacher began with the first grade level. These tests also indicated that Jack's instructional level should be a beginning third grade level with emphasis on comprehension exercises and vowel sounds.

Jack was next given tests of blends, vowels, double-vowels, and vowel-consonant sounds. On blends he was 95% correct; on beginning vowels (short sounds), he was 75% correct; on double vowel sounds, he was 80% correct; on vowel-consonant sounds he was 62% correct.

The teacher also gave Jack the "Diagnostic Test" which accompanies the *Reading Skilltext, Uncle Funny Bunny,* by Charles E. Merrill Books, Inc., a third grade reader. This test indicated that Jack is weakest in "getting the main ideas" and in "finding facts."

Jack was given an individual interest inventory. This indicated that Jack had anxieties regarding his family. It also indicated that he was interested in sports and liked school.

The Goodenough Draw-a-Man Test was also done by Jack. He made a score of 35 which indicates a Mental Age (MA) of 11-9. Jack also drew the House-Tree-Person picture. In interpreting the picture, the lack of ornamentation and shrubs around the house and bare branches on the trees indicated that Jack lacked interesting experiences and lacked affection. The tree seemed unrooted which suggests insecurity. On the man he drew, insecurity and inadequacy are suggested by his emphasis on the mid-line of the body, and his treatment of the body.

At the last meeting with Jack, he was given the Metropolitan Achievement Test in Reading for grades 3 and 4. His reading grade equivalent was 4.8 in Word Recognition and 4.9 in Reading Comprehension and Meaning.

VII. Diagnostic Formulation

A. Presenting Problem

Jack was doing unsatisfactory work in all his fifth grade classes due to the fact he could not read the fifth grade material. He was inattentive in school, daydreamed, and caused disturbances to get attention. These indicated that Jack was having mild emotional disturbances and feelings of insecurity as well as a negative self-concept.

In oral reading, Jack's specific retardation was mispronouncing unfamiliar words without looking for root words or parts, syllables, or trying to think if it makes sense.

In silent reading, Jack's specific retardation is in the following areas: 1. He lacks the ability to get the main idea. 2. He is inexperienced in arranging ideas—to note relationships and to organize what he has read. 3. He lacks ability to think clearly. 4. He needs training where he is weak as in vowel study and application, but not re-education in all the skills and abilities. 5. He needs training and reminding to do his work carefully and "think." He needs to learn to remember that he has a definite purpose for reading carefully.

His individual reading inventory indicates that his instructional level should be a beginning third grade level with emphasis on vowel sounds and on comprehension exercises.

B. Etiology (Causation)

Family problems seem to be causing part of Jack's problems. They have given him a poor self-concept and feelings of insecurity. This has caused him to have an irritable personality at home and school to get attention. It is also a cause for his short attention span and daydreaming.

School has caused classroom reading difficulties for although tests indicated from second grade on that he was failing in reading and needed help, he did not receive it, but was just passed on each year until his fourth grade teacher became concerned.

Tests indicated that Jack needed corrective or remedial reading instruction because his potential for reading was higher than his functional level.

C. Teacher's observation of child's behavior and performance at time of referral

At time of referral, Jack realized that he needed help in reading and he was anxious to learn. He came to the meetings with a good attitude, listened carefully, and tried to do his work carefully.

VIII. Treatment

A. Objectives

The chief objectives were to alleviate Jack's emotional anxieties and his reading difficulties. The aim was to talk to his mother and teacher concerning emotional problems, and to provide sequential materials that would steadily improve Jack's basic reading and study skills.

B. Purposes for these objectives

The purpose in relieving Jack's emotional anxiety was to help him to increase his attention span, to stop his class disturbances, and to lead to better study habits.

By helping him in his reading difficulties, he could learn to read nearer to his grade level and learn to enjoy reading for his own pleasure.

C. Detailed account of procedures and materials used to accomplish this

To accomplish these objectives, a corrective reading program was planned for Jack every Wednesday for one hour after school.

After testing, it was decided to use the Charles E. Merrill *Reading Skilltext, Uncle Funny Bunny,* a third grade reading level book. These stories are animal stories and Jack seemed interested in them. Before reading, each story was motivated by questions and discussion of the picture with the story. These stories had exercies that attack the comprehension problems Jack is weak in.

Five basic skill areas are covered in the exercises.

1. The pupil must learn to locate pertinent information, to recall facts previously read, skimming for important details, and rereading carefully to substantiate impressions.

The first exercise was finding facts. Here Jack completed statements of fact, answered questions about details in the story, and named or listed specific facts in the story.

2. The child must learn to grasp the main ideas in what he reads.

The second exercise was understanding ideas. The questions here were usually multiple choice. Since the answers were generally implied, Jack had to learn to read more attentively to clarify his thinking.

3. A child must develop the ability to organize material.

The third exercise, arranging ideas, helped Jack to learn to organize information in a variety of ways, such as rearranging ideas in sequence, to group and summarize facts, to divide stories logically into two or three main parts, and to select titles for these main parts.

4. The child must be able to make sound judgments on facts presented in their reading and draw valid conclusions and to recognize implications in regard to character.

In the fourth exercise, thinking clearly, Jack had to try to draw sound conclusions, appreciate feeling, and evaluate character.

5. The reader must acquire the basic skill to recognize, understand, and analyze words in and out of context.

In the fifth exercise, studying words, all words studied were from the story or directly related to words in the story. The meanings of key words in each story were developed. Jack learned to analyze the structure of words through the recognition of roots, prefixes and suffixes, compound words, singular and plural forms. It helped Jack to learn new words phonetically, how to recognize silent letters, and various vowel and consonant sounds as aids to pronunciation, and the basic dictionary skill of arranging words in alphabetical order.

To learn vowel sounds more effectively, the Lyons and Carnahans *Phonics We Use, Books C and D* also were used. These included exercises in listening to vowel sounds, and filling in blanks to complete exercises, and answering riddles with words containing specific vowel sounds.

The teacher made up her own questions and exercises for the use of vowel sounds and in giving directions to be followed, also.

To stimulate interest in reading, Jack read a few stories in the first book *The Sea Hunt,* from the *Deep Sea Adventure Series* by Harr, Wagner Publishing Company. He liked the stories but it was discontinued as his teacher planned to use it in his reading class.

Also to stimulate interest in reading, the teacher took Jack to the library where he browsed around and read some parts of some sport stories to the teacher. He also chose a book on football to take home.

To improve his oral reading, the teacher had Jack read aloud stories from *Uncle Funny Bunny* and *The Sea Hunt.* This was to encourage him to develop ease in oral reading and to begin analyzing his own reading difficulties.

To alleviate Jack's emotional difficulties, the teacher talked with his mother and discussed Jack's need for more attention and understanding by the whole family. Also, the teacher discussed his problems with his classroom teacher, and she had become aware of his needs and has given him help where needed. In the last few weeks, Jack had become better adjusted in school and is doing better work.

IX. Prognosis

Jack reads material on the third grade level fairly well. He needs to continue the work started so that he will continue his growth in his reading skills and interests. With interest in him and encouragement by both mother and classroom teacher, he should show good improvement.

X. Future Plans

Jack should have continued help for some time in the future. It is important for an interest to be shown in him and encouragement given to him so that he will continue to have better work habits and a good attitude toward his classroom work.

SECOND CASE SUMMARY

I. Identifying Data

A. Name: Bruce Bennett
B. Age: Eight
C. Sex: Male
D. Grade: Third
E. Ethnic Group: American Indian
F. Clinician: Mrs. Sally Johnson

II. Brief Description of Client

Bruce is a nice-looking boy of average size. He is an American Indian with brown eyes, shaggy brown hair, and regular features. His attitude toward reading and school is negative. Nevertheless, he usually applied himself well during the reading improvement program.

III. Problem

At the first interview with Bruce's parents, they were asked what they felt might be the cause of Bruce's reading difficulty. His mother responded that she believes Bruce feels insecure in his family. She offered no concrete reasons to support this statement and went on to say she and her husband have tried in many ways to show their love.

According to Bruce's first-grade teacher, he scored average on the reading readiness tests. He continued to do average until the work demanded more of an effort on his part. Then his progress halted. She recommended to Bruce's parents that he repeat first grade, but they refused to have him retained.

Bruce's present teacher questioned his first grade I.Q. of 111. Recently she gave him the Standord-Binet Intelligence Scale, and he recorded a score in the low 90's.

She also reported there is no carry-over in his reading skills. Bruce memorized dozens of sight-words on cards, but he could not identify them in context. He identifies initial consonant sounds when words are pronounced orally, but pays no attention to the initial consonant when he is trying to identify a word.

Bruce's third-grade teacher attributes his reading disability to his attitude of indifference toward school and reading and a low-average intelligence.

IV. Family Composition

Bruce is one of four adopted children. The oldest is a girl of sixteen. She is a blue-eyed, blond Caucasian. The other three children are American Indians. There is a girl two years older than Bruce and a four-year-old boy.

The parents are Caucasian and appear to be in their late thirties or early forties. The father is a foreman at a local company.

V. Contacts

Initial contact was made with Bruce on September 28th, 1967, and the final contact was made on December 18th, 1967. A total of 23 half hour sessions took place.

VI. Summary of Test Results

In first grade Bruce was given the Stanford-Binet Intelligence Scale and his I.Q. was 111. Last November, his third grade teacher administered the Stanford-Binet Scale again, and Bruce scored in the low 90's.

Last summer, Bruce participated in the summer school reading program. He received a grade equivalent score of 1.0 on the Gray Oral Reading Test. Teacher comments included "word-by-word reading" and "lots of repetition."

This teacher determined Bruce's reading level last September using the *Spache Diagnostic Reading Scales* published by the California Test Bureau. His instructional level was 1.6. However, Bruce only knew 74 sight-words on the Dolch Basic Sight Word Test. This placed him on a pre-primer level.

Several other informal tests were administered. An initial consonant sounds list was given to Bruce. He made 11 errors out of a possible 25. Bruce dictated two short experience stories. Out of a total of 87 words, he made 17 errors in his oral reading, giving him 80.5% accuracy.

His listening comprehension was tested by reading to him a selection from the Dolch Basic Book, *"Why" Stories,* which was on a 2-2 level. Bruce had 100% comprehension.

A test on consonant blend sounds was administered the first week in October. Bruce made 11 errors out of a possible 20. On a short vowel sounds test, he made 8 errors in the first 10 words. The remainder of the test was not given.

An attempt was made to determine Bruce's potential level in reading using selections from *Spache Diagnostic Reading Scales.* The results were very inconsistent. Therefore, this teacher feels that a valid potential level in reading was not established.

After the initial test of the Dolch Basic Sight Words, Bruce was tested two consecutive times at one month intervals. Whereas on the first testing, he made 63 errors, he made 37 errors on the second test. On the final sight word test he missed 19 words.

Several subtests of the *Doren Diagnostic Reading Test* were given to Bruce in early December. His areas of greatest difficulty were his inability to choose the correct beginning sound when supplying a word in context and his inability to recognize a word from vowels.

At the final reading session, Bruce was given the *California Achievement Test for Reading, Lower Primary.* Part I—Reading Vocabulary had four subtests. On *Word Form* he received a raw score of 15 out of a possible 25. His raw score on *Word Recognition* was 19 out of a possible 20. On the Meaning of Opposites he scored 10 out of 15, and his raw score on *Picture Association* was 12 out of a possible 15. His Reading Vocabulary grade placement was 1.9. Bruce's raw score on Part II—Reading Comprehension was 3 out of a possible 15. This gave him a grade placement of 1.3. This teacher feels that the Reading Comprehension scores were invalid, believing Bruce didn't read the short stories necessary to answer the questions.

VII. Diagnostic Formulation

Bruce's main problem was that of relearning all the developmental reading skills beginning at the preprimer level. There appear to be two important causative factors in Bruce's disability in reading. One major factor is that Bruce has been passed from first to second to third grade without ever learning first-grade reading skills.

The other possible cause may be some degree of emotional disturbance. At a parent-teacher conference in the fall, Bruce's mother related the fact that Bruce has been taking tranquilizers since he was four years old because of hyperactiveness and a nervous disorder which made him twitch. This nervous condition is no longer evident. Both parents have expressed concern over their inability to cope with Bruce successfully at home. As the school year has progressed, Bruce's teacher has also found him to be a discipline problem.

At the first reading session, Bruce was extremely quiet. He would not speak unless spoken to and then only uttered the minimum response. He didn't smile. He was cooperative, but not at all enthusiastic.

The teacher cannot determine whether Bruce's reading problem is caused by emotional disturbance or his apparent emotional disturbance is caused by his inability to read at grade level.

VIII. Treatment

Several objectives were formulated prior to beginning the reading improvement program with Bruce. The prime objective was for Bruce to develop self-confidence in his ability to read. Giving him a great amount of success initially was important, since Bruce had stated he disliked reading because he couldn't pronounce the words. The other important objectives involved the reteaching of the developmental reading skills beginning on a pre-primer level. Bruce did poorly on the Dolch Basic Sight Word Test. Also, on the informal reading analysis tests he proved weak in all areas of phonetic analysis skills. Since instructional time was limited and it was impossible to cover all areas of developmental reading skills adequately, major emphasis was given to teaching the basic sight words and initial consonant sounds.

To help develop self-confidence, Bruce was given much easy reading material. *Frog Fun* and *Tuggy,* pre-primers from the *Linguistic-Science Readers,* were chosen for the basic reading program. The teacher's manual was closely followed and adapted to Bruce's needs and age level. Most of "Building Skills" exercises given in the manual were utilized. They mainly emphasized auditory discrimination and initial consonant sounds. In addition to the easy reading found in these pre-primers, Bruce read two tradebooks which he seemed to enjoy. They were *Moonbeam at the Rocket Port* and *Cowboy Sam.* At every instructional period, time was allowed for Bruce to read orally. After oral reading, comprehension was always tested, either through informal discussion or specifically formulated questions on the literal and inferential levels.

To further motivate Bruce toward reading fluency, a tape recorder was used at one session. Bruce enjoyed listening to himself and easily pointed out his own reading difficulties.

Prior to motivating material to be read, vocabulary words were presented in context on 5 by 8 cards. Several sentences written in black with the new word inserted and underlined in red were given. The words were either used as in the selection to be read, or they were used in sentences pertaining to Bruce personally. These word cards were reviewed periodically.

Two charts were made for Bruce. One was a "Progress with Basic Sight Words" chart. After each sight word test was given, the results were recorded on the chart. The other chart was "Rocket Ship to the Moon," which indicated by little paste-on rocket ships, the books Bruce had read. At the end of the semester, Bruce took his charts home to show his parents and classroom teacher.

To help develop enjoyment in reading, Bruce was read to periodically. The materials used were Dolch *More Dog Stories,* Dolch *"Why" Stories, Reader's Digest Reading Skill Builder* (1-2), and *Humpty Dumpty's Magazine for Little Children.*

Throughout the reading improvement program, phonetic and structural analysis Bruce was given many exercises in phonetic and structural analysis using the following material: "Building Skills" from the *Teacher's Plan Book for the Pre-primers–Frog Fun, Tuggy* and *Pepper, Letters, Patterns and Drills, Beginning Steps in Phonics,* Developmental Reading Text Workbook, *Up and Away* (grade 1), and the *New Phonics Skilltext.*

Many of the exercises given were worked together. Those done independently by Bruce were always reviewed and corrected upon completion.

IX. Prognosis and Future Plans

Bruce needs much more help in learning the developmental skills of the second and third grades. If he is able to receive much individual attention and guidance in mastering these skills sequentially, he should be able to eventually read at or near his grade level.

Using a Child's Preferred Mode of Learning

Another important aspect of either corrective or remedial reading instruction can be using a child's preferred mode of learning. Some children seem to learn to read better through the use of one of their senses or a combination of two senses than they do by the use of some other one. For example, some children learn to read better through the use of a predominantly visual method while others learn to read better by an auditory method. Still other children, usually the slow-learning children, learn to read better through a kinesthetic (tracing) or VAKT method, while other children learn to read most effectively through the use of a combination method such as the visual and auditory methods.

Probably the most effective way for the teacher to determine a disabled reader's preferred mode of learning is by using the Learning Methods Test developed by Mills of Florida.[3] In giving the test, the teacher determines the child's instructional reading level following the directions in the manual and teaches a number of words on this level by using words printed on cards of various colors. She teaches the words by a visual, auditory, kinesthetic, or combination method. The teacher later gives a recall test of the words that she has taught and in this way she can determine the child's preferred mode of learning to read.

This book takes the position that the use of the child's preferred mode of learning should be just *one* method that is emphasized. Other approaches should also be used such as the language-experience approach, individualized reading, the initial teaching alphabet, or words in color depending on the child's difficulty and interests.

However, using the disabled reader's preferred mode of learning can be helpful in a reading improvement program. If he has been discovered to learn best by a *visual* method, word form clues such as configuration,

the use of the total word shape, the distinctive characteristics in words, ascending and descending letters, and other unique characteristics in words should be used as a major method of teaching word recognition. Occasionally the association of a word with the picture it represents can be used in the visual method.

If the child is found to learn best by an auditory method, phonetic analysis for word recognition should be emphasized in either the corrective or remedial reading program. At the beginning stage of phonetic analysis, auditory readiness activities such as rhyming words, giving words that begin with a certain consonant sound, or telling what consonant sounds certain objects begin with can be used. In the actual instruction of phonetic analysis, appropriate pages from basal reader workbooks, appropriate pages

---

[3] Robert E. Mills, *Learning Methods Test* (Fort Lauderdale, Florida: Mills Center Incorporated, 1964-1965).

from phonics workbooks, the extending skills and abilities part of a basal reader lesson, teacher-made phonics worksheets, or phonics games can be used.

If a disabled reader seems to learn to read best by a kinesthetic (VAKT) method, the Fernald Tracing Method, or the Gillingham-Stillman VAKT Method can be used. These two kinesthetic methods are somewhat similar except the Fernald Method emphasizes teaching words through the tracing of syllables, while the Gillingham-Stillman Method emphasizes teaching words through tracing single letters.

A brief example of how the Fernald Method is used is the following:

1. The disabled reader chooses a word that he wishes to learn to recognize, and the teacher writes it for him in manuscript or cursive handwriting, depending on his age, with a dark crayon on a piece of oaktag. The child then traces it with his index finger saying the word aloud in syllables as he traces it. He then attempts to write the word on a piece of paper without looking at the model. If he cannot do so, he retraces the word saying it aloud. He does this until he can write the word correctly. When he has written it, he copies it on an index card and files it in a box for further study. He also uses the word in a sentence or story.

2. At the second stage of remediation, the disabled reader writes each word that he wishes to learn to recognize, saying the word to himself in syllables as he writes it. He also writes each newly learned word on an index card and files it in his box. He uses the word in a sentence or story.

3. At the final stage of remediation, the disabled reader is able to read or write the words without tracing them or writing them from copy. He continues to file the newly learned words in his box and to use them in sentences and stories.[4]

More information about this method can be found in Fernald's book.[5] Fernald and her associates have reported very good results by using this method with moderately or severely disabled readers. Probably the main reasons it has been successful are that it is a novel way to learn to read and that it emphasizes left-to-right progression, syllabication, and reading for meaning.

---

[4]Grace M. Fernald, *Remedial Techniques in Basic School Subjects* (New York: McGraw-Hill Book Company, 1943).

[5]*Ibid.*

The Gillingham-Stillman Method[6] is more difficult to describe briefly, but the following is an account of how it is used:

> The child is to learn some short phonetically regular words. The teacher prints or writes the words to be learned with a dark crayon on a piece of oaktag. The child then isolates each sound of a word as he traces it with his index finger and later he attempts to blend the sound of the word. For example, if the word to be learned is "cat," the child traces it while he says "kuh-a-tuh" and then tries to blend the sounds into the word "cat." The child later tries to write the words from memory, and if he cannot do so, he traces the word letter by letter again.

The Gillingham-Stillman Method is recommended for use with children who have dyslexia as was described in Chapter II. This approach is good for them because it uses all their senses. However, in using this method with dyslexic children, the teacher should remember that each of the phonic generalizations must really be *overlearned* so that later confusion will not result. Therefore, this program must proceed at a very slow pace with *much* repetition and purposeful drill so that each concept is thoroughly learned before a new one is presented.

The Fernald Method seems better to use than the Gillingham-Stillman Method with children who learn best by a kinesthetic method since it uses syllables instead of isolated sounds. In the Gillingham-Stillman Method, the sounds are isolated and therefore distorted, making the blending of the word quite difficult. For example, it is difficult for most children to blend the word "cat" out of the sounds "kuh-a-tuh." However, the use of syllable blending in the Fernald Method does not cause a similar difficulty.

SUMMARY

Corrective reading instruction is provided by the regular classroom teacher sometime during the school day to those disabled readers who are not severely disabled and do not have emotional involvement related to their reading. Remedial reading instruction is given by a reading specialist in a reading clinic to

[6]Anna Gillingham and Bessie Stillman. *Remedial Training for Children with Specific Difficulty in Reading, Spelling and Penmanship.* (New York: Sackett and Williams Lithographing Corporation, 1940).

those children who are moderately or severely disabled and have some emotional disturbance related to their reading.

Most of the principles related to the developmental teaching of reading are equally applicable to corrective or remedial reading instruction. All of the principles of child growth and development should be considered in a reading improvement program. The program should build upon the child's present reading strengths, and the teacher must be sure that she establishes a good relationship with the child.

Probably the most single important characteristic either of corrective or remedial reading instruction is that it should be based specifically on diagnosed reading difficulties. Such reading difficulties may be a lack of mastery of the 220 basic sight words found on the Dolch Test, a weakness in phonetic analysis skills, a lack of mastery structural analysis skills, a weakness in the use of context clues, of difficulty with either literal or higher-type comprehension skills. The chapter illustrated ways in which each of these diagnosed difficulties can be corrected.

The teacher-pupil relationship is very important in determining if the child will make progress in the reading improvement program. The teacher should be warm and understanding, but also must command each child's respect.

Corrective or remedial reading instruction can be provided in either an individual or group setting. The chapter indicated that there may be advantages to interweaving the diagnosis and correction of reading difficulties. This chapter also gave many practical suggestions for using a disabled reader's interests in the reading improvement program, and suggested that the teacher should involve the child in diagnosing his reading difficulties and planning the reading improvement program. The chapter presented an example of an initial interview with the disabled reader and two illustrative case studies showing how an entire reading improvement program was conducted with two disabled readers.

It can be important to use a child's preferred mode of learning to read as *one* method for reading improvement. The Learning Methods Test can determine if a child learns to read best by a visual, auditory, kinesthetic, or combination method. The chapter also described the Fernald Tracing Method, a kinesthetic approach emphasizing the tracing of syllables, and the Gillingham-Stillman Method, an approach which emphasizes the tracing of individual letters and often is used with dyslexic children.

REFERENCES

Bond, Guy L. and Miles A. Tinker. *Reading Difficulties: Their Diagnosis and Correction.* New York: Appleton-Century-Crofts, 1967. Chapter 10.

Carter, Homer L. J. and Dorothy J. McGinnis. *Diagnosis and Treatment of the Disabled Reader.* New York: The Macmillan Company, 1970. Chapter 10.

Dechant, Emerald. *Diagnosis and Remediation of Reading Disability.* West Nyack, New York: Parker Publishing Company, 1968. Chapter 4.

Strang, Ruth. *Diagnostic Teaching of Reading.* New York: McGraw-Hill Book Company, 1969. Chapters 12 and 14.

Zintz, Miles V. *Corrective Reading.* Dubuque, Iowa: William C. Brown Company, Publishers, 1966. Chapter 4.

5

Correction of Word Recognition Difficulties

Chapter 3 described most of the useful standardized diagnostic reading tests which can be used to specifically diagnose word recognition difficulties. This chapter also illustrated how informal inventories in phonetic analysis, structural analysis, or context clues can be used as part of an individual reading inventory to diagnose specific word recognition difficulties.

Chapter 4 showed how either a corrective or remedial reading program must correct the specific word recognition difficulties which a disabled reader has. This chapter contains many practical suggestions about how to teach the word recognition skills of word form clues, phonetic analysis, structural analysis, picture and context clues, and dictionary usage. The chapter also gives suggestions of materials to correct deficiencies in the knowledge of word form clues, phonetic analysis, structural analysis, context clues, and dictionary usage.

Correcting Difficulties in the Use of Word Form Clues

The use of word form clues is one of the first word recognition skills that a child learns to use at the first-grade instructional reading level. Word form clues also are useful for adult readers. A disabled reader must know many words by sight before he can profit much from instruction in either phonetic or structural analysis. Each disabled reader should learn to recognize the 220 service words found in the Dolch Basic Sight Word Test. This test was discussed in Chapter 3, and difficulties in the knowledge of sight words can best be found by the use of this test. The 220 words found on the test make up 70% of the words found in an average first reader and 65% of the words found in a typical second reader. Therefore, the reader can see that a child must know most of these words to be able to make good improvement in reading.

A word form clue is used when a child gets the meaning or pronunciation of a word by using the total word instead of its parts. Configuration is one example of a word form clue:

Framing a word occurs when a child places his hands on either side of a word when it is written on the chalkboard or a piece of chart paper. Distinctive characteristics within words such as the double "o" in the word "book" or any pattern of tall and short letters also are examples of word form clues. Most of the words which a reader learns to recognize by another means such as phonetic or structural analysis eventually should become part of his stock of sight words. Most good readers see only the first several letters or the total shape of a word while they are reading and they do not stop to analyze the word.

Difficulties in recognizing the 220 words found on the Dolch Basic Sight Word Test are fairly common among disabled readers. Probably such a weakness is most common among disabled readers in the later primary or intermediate grades, but even some disabled readers at the junior and senior high school levels do not know all of these words. There are a number of ways to build a disabled reader's sight word bank in either a corrective or remedial reading program.

The Fernald Tracing Method which was described in detail in Chapter 4 can sometimes effectively be used to teach any of the sight words which are particularly difficult for a child to learn in some other way. Usually this method should not be used with all of the sight words which a child needs to learn, but only with those words which give a disabled reader particular trouble. As was described in detail in Chapter 4, this method involves the child's tracing a word from left to right while saying it aloud in syllables and later writing the word without looking at the copy.

Generally, it is better to teach the sight words in context instead of isolation. Obviously, a child meets words in context when he is reading. One such activity has the teacher write a sentence containing the sight word that she wishes to teach on a long piece of oaktag with the sight word written in red and the remainder of the words in the sentence written in black (Figure 5-1). The child learns to identify the sight word in context and is able to use context clues along with word form clues. Such practice should be spaced, and such an activity should not last more than about ten minutes in any one-hour corrective or remedial reading session.

John has three very GOOD friends.

FIGURE 5-1

Sight words also can be taught effectively by using dictated language-experience stories. The disabled reader can dictate a language-experience story which the teacher prints in manuscript handwriting or types for him on a primary or regular typewriter. The teacher can then make a window card out of a three by five inch index card, and the window in this card is placed over each sight word which the child is trying to learn (Figure 5-2).

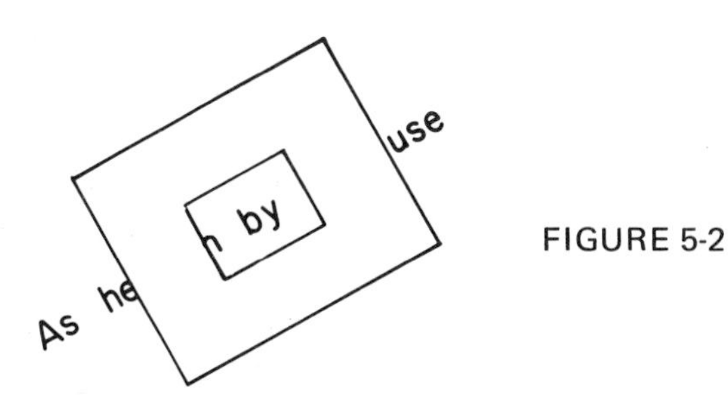

FIGURE 5-2

Any sight words that the teacher is trying to teach can be printed or typed on a small index card, and these words may later by filed by the disabled reader in a small metal box or any other available type of box such as a shoe box. The child then can place the word cards in envelopes depending on which alphabet letter each word begins with and place all the envelopes in alphabetical order in their box. The disabled reader can later review all the words in his box on his own at spaced intervals and add to his sight word bank in this way.

A game containing the 220 service words from the Dolch Basic Sight Word Test can be used to teach or reinforce the learning of sight words. The Dolch Basic Sight Vocabulary Cards teach the 220 service words in a game setting. These word cards can be purchased from the Garrard Press of Champaign, Illinois. The Garrard Press also has a set of illustrated word cards presenting the 95 nouns which are common in primary-grade reading materials. These word cards are the Dolch Picture-Word Cards. In either case, the words are presented in isolation so they should not be used as a sole method of teaching the sight words. In playing a game with either of these word cards, time periods of ten to fifteen minutes probably are best. The teacher and the disabled reader or two disabled readers can use these cards as one activity in a corrective or remedial reading session.

The teacher or the disabled reader can make his own set of word cards to help in building the child's stock of sight words. The cards should be made from oaktag or cardboard which cannot be seen through. The word can be printed on each card on one side with either a magic marker, felt-tipped pen, or a crayon. On the other side of each card a picture and the word are also placed. The child can study each word using the picture as a guide. For verbs and function words the child must draw a picture which represents the word to him, while nouns are very easy for the child to illustrate. In working with these word cards, it is important for the teacher and disabled reader to concentrate on learning or reviewing a few words at a time thoroughly. If too many words are studied at the same time, the disabled reader probably will not learn or review each one sufficiently to avoid mixing them up later. Short enjoyable practice periods which are about a ten minute part of any reading improvement session are better than one longer practice session, since this can become very boring for a disabled reader.

Several machines also can be used to either reinforce or to

present sight words. Examples of such machines are *The Language Master* (manufactured by Bell and Howell Company), the *TTC Magnetic Card Reader* (manufactured by the Teaching Technology Corporation), and the *e f i Audio Flashcard System* (manufactured by Educational Futures, Incorporated). Each of these machines use large cards which have strips of magnetic tape mounted on them. The disabled reader looks at the card, tries to recognize the word, places the card in the machine and listens through earphones as a voice says the word for him. The disabled reader's identification of the word also can be recorded and played back. Prerecorded cards, printed cards, and blank cards can be purchased for any of these three machines.

It is important for a disabled reader to see his progress in learning to recognize the 220 service words on the Dolch Basic Sight Word Test in some very concrete manner. Such extrinsic motivation often is not recommended for use with average and good readers, but it often is what a disabled reader needs to have to convince himself that he really is making progress in reading improvement. Different teachers have developed different con-

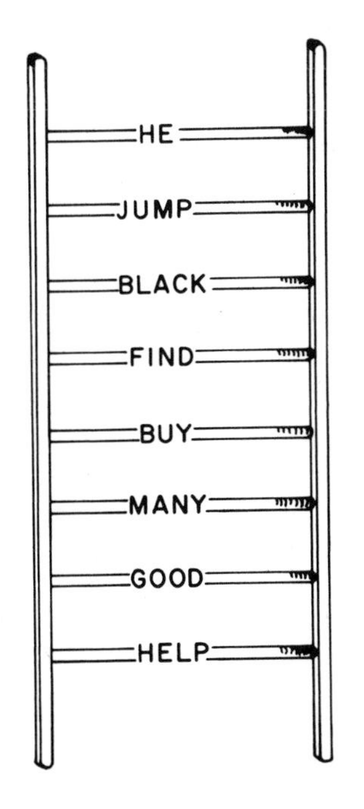

FIGURE 5-3

crete ways of doing this. Some teachers make word ladders where each new sight word learned becomes a higher rung on the ladder, as shown in Figure 5-3.

Other teachers make various kinds of charts, like a balloon added to the chart with each new sight word written on it or a rocket ship which moves higher on the chart for each sight word learned.

To summarize, there are several ways in which the teacher can present and review sight words. Generally, she should teach the words in context most of the time, although it can be acceptable to isolate them at times. Each sight word should be completely mastered by a disabled reader, and the teacher should work with few enough of them at a time to be sure that the child learns them completely and does not confuse them. It also is more effective to study sight words for short time periods with much meaningful practice instead of studying them for longer periods of time with less practice.

Correcting Difficulties with Phonetic Analysis Skills

Phonetic analysis is one of the most important word recognition techniques—most reading specialists feel that phonetic analysis along with the use of context clues certainly is the most useful word recognition skill. Phonetic analysis can be defined either as the association of sound and symbol or the association of phoneme and grapheme. In either case, phonetic analysis consists of the sounding of consonants and vowels to get the pronunciation and meaning of an unknown word.

There are two types of phonetic analysis skills that are taught in today's reading materials. They are analytic phonetic analysis and synthetic phonetic analysis. The use of analytic phonetic analysis is begun when an entire word is looked at by the reader. He then divides it into syllables if it is a longer word (which is a structural analysis skill) and assigns the sounds to the various letters within each syllable. He then blends the syllables into the whole word to get its pronunciation. Hopefully, it is a word which is in his oral language vocabulary and he is able to understand it in the context of the sentence in which he found it. As an example, the word "butter" would be sounded as "bŭt/ter."

On the other hand, synthetic phonetic analysis consists of the building up of a word by using the sounds which each letter in the word has. For example, the word "bat" would be blended as "buh-a-tuh." In this case the consonant sounds usually become distorted since a consonant cannot be said in isolation without adding a vowel sound also.

The phonetic analysis techniques which are presented in the basal reader manuals always are analytic, while the phonetic analysis skills presented in different formal phonics programs are either of the analytic or synthetic type. Most reading specialists believe that analytic phonetic analysis is the most meaningful for children in the elementary school since the analysis is begun with a whole word—an example of Gestalt psychology. In analytic analysis the consonant sounds are not distorted; and since the child is working with larger units in the words, he is not so likely to become bogged down with the small details.

Presently most reading specialists recommend using inductive teaching of phonetic analysis since this is related to the use of the discovery method which is used in modern mathematics. In inductive teaching of phonetic analysis, the teacher first choses a phonic rule which she wants a child to learn. She then chooses five or more words which will illustrate this rule very clearly. She then places the words on the chalkboard or on a sheet of paper and asks the child to tell her what each word is. The teacher asks the child if he can see anything similar about the five words and, by guiding his thinking carefully, she helps him to state the rule. The child states the rule in his own words and the teacher usually helps him to clarify the rule by helping him to restate it. Inductive teaching of phonetic analysis generally is thought to be more meaningful and practical for a child since he has to think about the rule for himself instead of merely verbalizing it without understanding it after the teacher has stated it for him.

A disabled reader should receive careful systematic instruction only in those areas of phonetic analysis skills in which he was found to be weak by the use of a diagnostic reading test, an informal phonics inventory, or teacher observation while the child is reading orally from many different kinds of materials. A number of disabled readers are fairly proficient in the use of consonant sounds, particularly in the use of the initial consonant sounds. However, they often are weak in the knowledge of vowel sounds since the vowels have so many different sounds, and the sounds are quite similar unless a child has very good auditory discrimination. A number of disabled readers also have difficulty in auditory blending or in putting sounds and syllables together to form words which they can recognize.

If a disabled reader is weak in nearly all areas of phonetic analysis, he first must have training in auditory discrimination or in hearing the likenesses and differences in sounds. Good auditory discrimination is a readiness skill to insure later success in phonetic analysis. There are a number of activities which can be used to develop good auditory discrimination ability for a disabled reader who needs it. Any rhyming activities such as listening to the teacher read nursery rhymes or playing many kinds of rhyming games may help to develop ability in auditory discrimination. The following are several examples of simple rhymes which the disabled reader may finish orally:

Jack is a boy
Who likes to play with his________________.
The fat funny clown
Is going to________________.
Billy, can you look
At my nice picture________________.
The old red fox
Got caught in a________________.
The cute little pup
Can learn how to sit________________.

The teacher also can present a series of objects that begin with the same consonant sound and ask the disabled reader to tell her what these objects are. The teacher then can ask him how these objects are alike, and the disabled reader can tell her that they all begin with the same sound. A list of objects for the sound of "b" are a ball, a basket, a boat, and a bell. The teacher can also ask the child if he can name some things which begin with the same sound as his name. As an example, a child named Mark could name the words monkey, man, money, and magazine.

The teacher also can present a group of objects, all of which begin with the same sound except one of them, and ask the disabled reader to tell her which one of them begins with a different sound. The teacher can present the objects top, table, candy, toy, and truck, and then ask the child to tell her which of them begins with a different sound than the others. The teacher also can present a list of words and ask the disabled reader to tell her which of the words begins with a different sound than the others. As an example, she can say the following words and ask the disabled reader which of them begins with a different sound than the other ones: bakery, bark, beautiful, be, bump, baby, dog, balloon, and butter.

The teacher can also take the disabled reader on a "sensitizing experience" to help promote good auditory discrimination. In a sensitizing experience the teacher and child can take a walk around the school neighborhood on a nice day, and the child is asked to listen just as carefully as he can for all the different sounds which he can hear. On a typical walk he may hear the songs of various birds, hear the wind whistling through the trees, or hear the sounds his own footsteps make on the sidewalk. A sensitizing experience can help him to become more aware of the sounds which he hears around him.

There are also some records available which can be used to develop auditory discrimination ability. These records present various types of sounds and ask the child to identify the sounds to promote his auditory discrimination. Some examples of records are as follows:

Spotlight on Sound Effects by Pickwock International Incorporated, Long Island City, New York.
Sounds Around Us by Scott, Foresman and Company.
Sounds for Young Readers by Educational Records Sales.
Auditory Training by The Greystone Corporation.
Muffin in the City, Muffin in the Country, Noisy Book, Muffin at the Seashore by E. M. Hale Company, Eau Claire, Wisconsin.
Listening Time Albums by Webster Publishing Company.
Let's Listen by Ginn and Company.
Phonics for Children by Audio-Education, American Book Company.

For a disabled reader who has sufficient readiness in auditory discrimination to be able to make good progress in beginning phonetic analysis skills, the teacher usually can make a plan for teaching these skills by consulting the basal reader manuals of any good reading series. All basal reader series present the consonant sounds first, since the reading specialists who author these series state that consonant sounds are more stable than are vowel sounds. Consonants are often in the left-hand side of the word and left-to-right progression therefore is stressed which may eliminate later reversals. The short and long vowel sounds generally are presented next and later phonic elements such as consonant blends, consonant digraphs, diphthongs, and phonograms are presented. Analytic phonetic analysis is stressed, and one of the early phonetic analysis skills taught is consonant substitution or the changing of "bump" to "jump."

Therefore, the manuals of any good basal reader series are considered to be the best resource for any teacher in a reading improvement program to use in deciding how to teach the various phonetic analysis skills. In the basal reader manuals phonetic analysis skills are outlined carefully and sequentially, and the teacher can refer to the manuals which represent the instructional reading level of the disabled reader. Of course, the teacher should teach only those phonetic analysis skills which the child has been found to need, such as the long vowel sounds or the short vowel sounds. The teacher should use a basal reader manual only as a guide in deciding how to teach the phonetic analysis skills, but the manuals do provide a very good guide in the area. The teacher can also use the basal reader workbooks on the disabled reader's instructional reading level to reinforce the phonetic analysis skills which she has taught in some other way. Only the workbook pages which reinforce the phonetic analysis skills which the disabled reader needs should be used. Basal reader workbooks should *not* be used in this case in cover-to-cover way. The following is a comprehensive list of the basal reader series which currently are in wide use in elementary schools:

Alice and Jerry Basic Reading Program. Harper and Row, Publishers, 49 East 33rd Street, New York 10016.

Bank Street Readers. The Macmillan Company, 866 Third Avenue, New York 10022.

Betts Basic Readers. American Book Company, 300 Pike Street, Cincinnati, Ohio 45202

Catholic University of America Faith and Freedom Series. Ginn and Company, Waltham, Massachusetts 02154.

Chandler Language-Experience Readers. Chandler Publishing Company, 124 Spear Street, San Francisco, California 94105.

City Schools Reading Program. Follett Educational Corporation, 1010 West Washington Boulevard, Chicago, Illinois 60607.

Developmental Reading Series. Lyons and Carnahan, Incorporated, 307 East 25th Street, Chicago, Illinois 60616.

Easy Growth in Reading Series. Holt, Rinehart and Winston, Incorporated, 383 Madison Avenue, New York 10017.

Get Ready to Read Series. The Bobbs-Merrill Company, 4300 West 62nd Street, Indianapolis, Indiana 46268.

Ginn Basic Readers. Ginn and Company, Waltham, Massachusetts, 02154.

Harper and Row Basic Reading Program. Harper and Row Publishers, 49 East 33rd Street, New York 10016.

Learning to Read Series. Silver, Burdett and Company, Box 2000, Morristown, New Jersey 07960.

The Macmillan Readers. The Macmillan Company, 866 Third Avenue, New York 10022.

The New Basic Readers. Scott, Foresman and Company, Glenview, Illinois 60025.

The Quinlan Basic Readers. Allyn and Bacon, Incorporated, 150 Tremont Street, Boston, Massachusetts 02111.

Reading Essential Series. Steck-Vaughn Company, P.O. Box 2028, Austin, Texas 78767.

Reading for Interest Series, Revised. D. C. Heath and Company, 285 Columbus Avenue, Boston, Massachusetts 02116.

Reading for Meaning Series, Revised. Houghton Mifflin Company, 2 Park Street, Boston, Massachusetts 02107.

Sheldon's Basic Reading Series. Allyn and Bacon, Incorporated, 150 Tremont Street, Boston, Massachusetts 02111.

SRA Basic Reading Series. Science Research Associates, Incorporated, 259 East Erie Street Chicago, Illinois 60611.

Winston Basic Readers. Holt, Rinehart and Winston, Incorporated, 383 Madison Avenue, New York 10017.

Special phonics workbooks also can be used as a source of materials to use in developing phonetic analysis skills. Such special phonics workbooks are found in the basal reader series of some publishers at the present time. There also are other phonics workbooks that can be used in a reading improvement program. These special phonics workbooks should be used in the same way that was described for the workbooks of the basal reader series. Workbooks should be chosen on the disabled reader's instructional reading level, and only those pages or exercises which teach or reinforce the phonetic analysis skills which the child needs should be used. As an example, if the disabled reader was found to be weak in the knowledge of short vowel sounds, only those pages or exercises that deal with short vowel sounds should be used. Some special materials to develop ability in phonetic analysis are as follows:

Durrell-Murphy Phonics Practice Program–Harcourt, Brace and World Incorporated, 757 Third Avenue, New York 10017

Speech-to-Print Phonics–Harcourt, Brace and World, Incorporated, 757 Third Avenue, New York 10017

New Phonics Skilltexts Series–Charles E Merrill Books, Incorporated, Columbus, Ohio 43216

Phonics We Use–Lyons and Carnahan, 407 E. 25th Street, Chicago, Illinois 60616

Phonetic Keys to Reading–The Economy Company, Oklahoma City, Oklahoma 73135

Phonovisual–Phonovisual Products, Incorporated, Box 5625, Washington, D. C. 20016

Breaking the Sound Barrier–The MacMillan Company, 866 Third Avenue, New York 10022

Hay-Wingo Method–J. B. Lippincott Company, East Washington Square, Philadelphia, Pennsylvania 19105

Open Court Method–Open Court Publishing Company, LaSalle, Illinois 61501.

Of course, the teacher in a reading improvement program also can construct her own worksheets to reinforce the phonics skills which she has taught to a disabled reader. She can construct worksheets by using the manuals of the appropriate grade levels of a basal reader series or the appropriate pages from either a basal reader workbook or a special phonics workbook as a guide. Such worksheets can be very useful in any reading improvement program because they are individually constructed to fit the child's particular needs, and even his interests can be used by the teacher in them. As an example, if a boy is interested in making airplane models, sentences actually pertaining to this interest can be used to teach any specific phonetic analysis skill. Of course, only those phonetic analysis skills in which the child was found to be weak should be presented or reinforced by using a teacher-made worksheet.

There also are commercially available games which the teacher can use to reinforce the phonetic analysis skills which she has presented to a disabled reader in the reading improvement program. Such games can be played with the child or with several disabled readers for about ten minutes in a one hour corrective or remedial reading session. Of course, a phonics game should be used as only one way of reinforcing the phonetic analysis skills which have been taught, and the game should be played to reinforce the skills not just because it is an enjoyable game. Some examples of commercially available phonics games are as follows:

> *Phonetic Quizmo*—Milton Bradley Company, Springfield, Massachusetts 01101
>
> *Consonant Lotto*—Garrard Press, Champaign, Illinois 61820
>
> *Vowel Lotto*—Garrard Press, Champaign, Illinois 61820
>
> *Phonics We Use Learning Games Kit*—Lyons and Carnahan, 407 East 25th Street Chicago, Illinois 60616
>
> *Phono-Word Wheels*—Steck-Vaughn Company, P. O. Box 2028, Austin, Texas 78767
>
> *Go Fish*—Remedial Education Press, Kingsbury Center, 2138 Bancroft Place, NW, Washington, D.C. 20008
>
> *Vowel Dominoes*—Remedial Education Press, Kingsbury Center, 2138 Bancroft Place, NW, Washington, D. C. 20008
>
> *Phonic Rummy*—Kenworthy Educational Service, Incorporated, P. O. Box 3031, 138 Allen Street, Buffalo, New York 14205
>
> *ABC Game*—Kenworthy Educational Service, Incorporated, P. O. Box 3031, 138 Allen Street, Buffalo, New York 14205

The teacher or disabled reader, or both of them together, can construct their phonics games. The phonics games should mainly be used to reinforce the phonics skills which were taught in a reading improvement session and should be used for only about ten minutes in a corrective or remedial reading session. Some examples of home-constructed phonics games are as follows:

> *Fishing*—A word, phrase, or sentence is printed on fish which have been cut out of cardboard or oaktag. A paper clip is attached to each fish, and the child picks up a fish with a horseshoe magnet attached to a ruler with a string. If the child can read the word, sentence, or phrase, he can keep the fish. Two children can play this game together, and the winner is the child that has the most fish.
>
> *Darts*—A dart set is used in this game. Cards with a phonogram on each one are pasted to the target, and an initial consonant is pasted on each dart. If the child reads the word formed when his dart hits a phonogram, he scores a point.

Spin the Pointer—Words are placed at the outside of a circle, and the child tries to read the word at which the pointer stops. A success in saying the word is scored as a hit and a failure is an out and the score is kept in terms of runs. By making slits into which word cards can be inserted, the same circle and pointer can be used several times.

Racing—A race track can be drawn and divided into boxes, and a word is placed in each box. Each child has a cutout automobile of a different color. When a child gets his turn, he spins his pointer indicating a move of one, two, three, or four boxes. If he can read the word, he can move his automobile ahead that many spaces; if not, he has to wait for his next turn.

Phonic Strips—Three horizontal slits are made across a four by six inch index card close together and in line. Three other slits are made right under them. A number of thin strips are made by cutting up another index card at the right width so they can be threaded through the slits to expose only a small part of the strip. On one strip a number of initial consonants can be printed in a vertical row, on the second strip medial vowels, and on the third strip some common word endings. By inserting the strips and moving them up and down, many different words can be made.

Correcting Difficulties in Structural Analysis Skills

Structural analysis is a word recognition skill involving the use of word parts to help a reader get the meaning and pronunciation of words. Therefore, it consists of the use of base or root words, prefixes and suffixes, syllabication, accent, and compound words.

Structural analysis also involves phonetic analysis skills since word parts must be sounded before they can be blended together to form a total word. In analyzing an unknown word, structural analysis usually should be used before phonetic analysis since the word parts in structural analysis are larger and therefore the word can be analyzed more quickly.

These skills normally are taught in the first grade instructional reading level when a child learns to attach a few simple suffixes or endings to the base words which he has learned as sight words. In the first reader level, a child learns to attach the suffixes "s," "ed," and "ing" to the word "jump" to make the new words "jumps," "jumped," and "jumping." At the later primary-grade reading levels other suffixes are presented which are added to the base words a child has learned either as sight words or by analyzing them phonetically. Examples of such suffixes are "y," "ly," "en," "es," "er," and "en."

At the later primary and intermediate-grade instructional reading levels prefixes and their meanings are presented. The study of the meaning of various prefixes can help a disabled reader add to his stock of vocabulary words if the child really wants to learn them. The following are some common prefixes and their meaning:

ab	from
ad, ap, at	to
be	by
con, com, col	with
de	from
dis	apart, not
en, em	in
ex	out
in, im	in, into
in, im	not
ob, of, op	against, away, from
pre, pro	before, in front of
re	back
post	behind
super	over, above
trans	across
sub	under
un	not

Structural analysis generalizations should usually be taught in an inductive manner much as was described for phonic generalizations. As an example the teacher can place five or more words on the chalkboard which are designed to illustrate a rule. She then can help the child spell each of the new words with the suffix attached to them and helps the child to state the structural rule for himself. The teacher may write the following words:

baby	babies
party	parties
pony	ponies
lady	ladies
city	cities

The child may state this structural generalization in the following way: "When you have a word ending with y with a consonant in front of the y, you change the y to i before you add es." Inductive teaching of a structural generalization is supposed to help the child to understand and remember the rule better. A list of several structural generalizations which can be taught inductively if a disabled reader has been found to need them is found in Appendix VII.

Readiness for dividing words into syllables usually is begun at the first reader level when the teacher pronounces a word like "butter" and asks the child how many parts he hears in this word. Readiness for syllabication also can involve a child's tapping out or clapping the number of syllables or parts he hears in a list of words which the teacher pronounces for him. For example, for a disabled reader on the early third grade instructional reading level, the teacher can pronounce the following list of words and ask him to clap his hands once for each part of the word that he hears:

nibble–two claps	beautiful–three claps
valley–two claps	back–one clap
man–one clap	hungrier–three claps
country–two claps	bottle–two claps

Actual instruction in dividing words into syllables usually takes place at the later third grade instructional reading level. There are a number of structural analysis rules dealing with syllabication that should be learned so that a child can use syllabication as one word recognition technique. These rules deal with dividing words between two consonants which are alike, between two consonants which are different, between a vowel and a consonant, and between two vowels. A list of these rules of syllabication is found in Appendix VII.

The rules of syllabication should be taught to a child in an inductive manner with the teacher putting words designed to illustrate the rule on the chalkboard or a sheet of paper and helping him to discover the rule and state it for himself in his own words. As an example, the teacher can place the following words on the chalkboard or on a sheet of paper:

ladder	rubber	supper
butter	better	

The child should be able to state this rule in about the following way: 'When there are two consonants together which are alike, you divide the word between these two consonants."

Structural analysis also deals with accent, and accent is presented inductively a little later than syllabication since these two skills are quite related. A list of accent generalizations is found in Appendix VII. Structural analysis also included the use of compound words that are introduced at the first reader level when a child learns to recognize words such as "cowboy," "fireman," and "playground." A child learns to divide a compound word between the two small words it is composed of a little later.

When any child meets an unknown word, he should first try to use context clues to get the pronunciation and meaning of the word. Next he should use his structural analysis skills, next the phonetic analysis skills, and only as a last resource should he use his dictionary skills. Structural analysis skills should be presented to only those disabled readers who have shown a clear evidence of weakness in them on a standardized diagnostic reading test or on the structural analysis inventory which was given as part of the individual reading inventory. For most disabled readers the major emphasis should probably be placed on learning how to divide words into syllables and how to blend the syllables together to form words. However, syllabication first rests upon the child's knowledge of phonetic analysis skills. Therefore, syllabication probably should receive the most emphasis for a disabled reader who already has adequate knowledge of phonetic analysis.

The teacher in a reading improvement program probably can get the most useful suggestions for teaching any of the structural analysis skills from the appropriate grade level book of any of the basal reader manuals of the series listed earlier in this chapter. The teacher must choose the structural analysis skills that she has found the child to be weak in and get suggestions about how to teach and reinforce these skills from the appropriate basal reader teacher's manual. Obviously only those pages of the appropriate basal reader workbooks should be used which give worthwhile reinforcement of the structural analysis skills which the teacher has taught to the disabled reader.

Of course, the teacher can construct her own worksheets to help present or review the structural analysis skills which a disabled reader needs to learn. She can use a basal reader manual or a basal reader workbook as a guide, but she can individually make the worksheets to reflect the child's special interests so that he will have more motivation to use them than he otherwise would.

The Fernald Tracing Method, which was described in detail in Chapter 4, can also be of use in teaching syllabication. This method emphasizes the pronouncing, tracing, and writing of the syllables in words and then blending the syllables together to form words. Therefore, it can be useful for a disabled reader who is weak in syllabication especially when the teacher is first presenting this skill. The pronouncing and tracing of the syllables may not be necessary for an extended time period, but can be useful for a time.

There are a few commercially available games to teach various structural analysis skills, and the teacher and child together can also make some aids in this area. A brief list of some games is as follows:

Phono–Word Wheels–Steck-Vaughan Company, P. O. Box 2028, Austin, Texas 78767

Webster Word Wheels–Webster Division of McGraw-Hill Book Company, Manchester Road, Manchester, Missouri 64011

Word Structor–H. Benson, 2121 Westbury Court, Brooklyn, New York 11225

The Syllable Game–Garrard Publishing Company, Champaign, Illinois 61820

Lucky Wheel–Two circles of different sizes are fastened together by brads through their centers so that each can be moved freely. On the smaller circle base words are printed and on the outer circle either prefixes or suffixes are printed. By rotating the outer circle, many new words can be formed.

Correcting Difficulties in the Use of Picture and Context Clues

Picture clues are one of the word recognition techniques which a child learns to use at the first grade instructional reading level. Picture clues involve the association of a picture and a word or the use of a picture to give clues to an unknown word on the same page or a nearby page. They receive the most emphasis in the early stages of reading instruction, but continue to receive some emphasis at the later elementary grade reading levels perhaps especially in the content fields of social studies and science.

Context clues are used when a reader tries to get the meaning of an unknown word from the way it is used in the rest of the sentence, paragraph, or possibly the passage. Context clues usually are the first word recognition skill which a reader should use in getting the meaning of an unknown word. Most reading specialists believe that the use of context clues and phonetic analysis (especially the initial consonant sound) in combination are the single most effective word recognition technique.

Constance McCullough of San Francisco State College has put context clues into four groups. She calls the idea clue when a reader uses his own experiences to help him get a word's meaning and the contrast clue when a reader gets the meaning of an unknown word from its contrast with a known word in a sentence. Presentation clues are used when the position of the word in the sentence gives the major clue, and sentence sequence clues are used when the unknown word is derived from the order in which the sentences are found in the paragraph.[1]

Obviously, the teacher in any reading improvement program cannot use a test score to determine if a child understands how to use picture clues. She must discover this in an informal way by asking a disabled reader to tell her about some of the pictures in the appropriate grade level of the basal readers or tradebooks which he is reading. A child may have difficulty with the use of picture clues if he is seriously disabled in reading or has an instructional reading level on the first reader level. The teacher can show the child how to use pictures to help him get the meaning of unknown words on the same page or on a nearby page. She also can teach him how to interpret pictures critically and creatively. In this kind of picture interpretation, the child must go beyond the picture itself and project himself into it in some way.

The teacher can determine if a disabled reader needs instruction in how to use context clues in several ways. She can discover this kind of weakness while listening to the child read orally from the graded reading paragraphs of the individual reading inventory which was illustrated in Chapter 3. If he supplies words for unknown words which do not make sense in the sentence, he probably does not know how to use context clues effectively or is not concerned about reading for meaning. The teacher also can discover a weakness in the use of context clues from a context

---

[1]Constance M. McCullough and Miles A. Tinker. *Teaching Elementary Reading.* New York: Appleton-Century-Crofts, 1968, pp. 164-168.

clue inventory which can be given as part of the individual reading inventory. The teacher also can determine a difficulty in the use of context clues by noticing how well the child uses them when he is reading to her orally during the first stages of a reading improvement program.

Of course, a disabled reader should be given direct instruction in learning how to use context clues effectively only if he has shown a deficiency in the area. For a child who is reading at the readiness or early first reader level, the use of oral context as provided by the teacher and the use of the initial consonant sound can be very helpful in deveolping the use of context clues. This method and the materials which illustrate it were developed by McKee and Harrison of Colorado State College and are published in a series called the *Reading for Meaning Series,* Houghton Mifflin Company, 2 Park Street, Boston, Massachusetts 02107.

In developing competence in the use of context clues the basal reader manuals at the appropriate instructional grade level provide a good source of material for the teacher in any reading improvement program. The examples found in the basal readers give the teacher guidelines as to how she can present context clues. Many disabled readers do not understand why context clues are important or how they can be used unless they receive direct instruction in their use. Otherwise, context clues are thought by many children to be just a way of letting them guess wildly at the meaning of an unknown word.

Some of the pages in the appropriate basal reader workbooks also can be used to reinforce the effective use of context clues. Only those workbook pages dealing with context clues should be used for this purpose, and those pages mainly should be used to reinforce the teaching which has already been done.

The teacher also can construct her own worksheets to help her teach or reinforce the use of context clues. She can use either the basal reader teacher's manuals or the basal reader workbook pages as a guide, and she can individualize the worksheets by using the disabled reader's special interests to motivate him. Several examples of sentences illustrating the use of context clues at the third-grade instructional reading level are as follows:

With a big ______________ on his face, Mark ran up to the Indian boy.

growl
group
grin

The man pushed his big ______________ far back on his head as he stood there thinking.
hat
help
happy

The ______________ rested his weary legs by the fire in the living room.
peddler
party
pocket

Do you know where I can get a map of the ______________ ?
wall
world
with

He could use the serape as an overcoat on cold days and as a ______________ on cold nights.
blanket
blue
blend

Wide reading of easy interesting material also can be of help in developing a disabled reader's ability to use context clues effectively. Such reading practice should be motivated and should be on the child's independent or free reading level. It should be from materials which interest him and in which he has had some choice. Such wide reading can be from basal reader stories, supplementary books, trade books, reference books, and children's newspapers and magazines.

Correcting Difficulties in Dictionary Usage

When a child meets an unknown word while reading, the use of either a dictionary or glossary should be the final word recognition technique which he tries to apply. Therefore, ability to use a dictionary probably is not of major importance for most moderately disabled readers in the elementary school. However, some mildly or moderately disabled readers in the intermediate grades or junior high school should receive direct instruction in dictionary usage as part of the reading improvement program. However, even these children should be taught that the dictionary should be used only as a last resort when they meet an unknown word.

Dictionary skills are quite difficult for most children in the elementary school to learn. Dictionary skills consist of the abilities of alphabetizing, phonetic analysis, the use of guide words and the choosing of the correct dictionary definition for use in the context where the unknown word was found.

Dictionary readiness can be begun in the later first reader or second reader instructional level when a child is asked to put a list of five words in alphabetical order by the first letter:

baby	goat	quit
donkey	ice cream	party
apple	jump	mother
elephant	farm	over
candy	happy	never

Dictionary readiness also can include using a commercially available picture dictionary or pictionary, each page of which contains a letter and several words or pictures of objects beginning with that letter. Several commercially available picture dictionaries are as follows:

Picture Book Dictionary by Dilla MacBean. Childrens Press, Incorporated, 1224 West Van Buren Street, Chicago, Illinois 60617

Young Reader's Color-Picture Dictionary for Reading by Margaret Parke. Grosset and Dunlap, 51 Madison Avenue, New York, New York 10010

At the dictionary readiness level a child also can construct his own picture dictionary which is made from sheets of manila paper on which he has printed one alphabet letter. On the same page, the child then prints words beginning with this alphabet letter and draws pictures or cuts pictures out of a magazine beginning with the same letter (Figure 5-4). He then compiles all twenty-six pages in alphabetical order and makes an interesting cover for the picture dictionary.

Actual instruction in using a simplified or junior dictionary usually comes at the later third-grade instructional reading level. One way for the teacher in a reading improvement program to learn how to teach dictionary skills is to carefully examine a simplified dictionary. The disabled reader needs much direct instruction in using alphabetical sequence, in applying his phonetic analysis skills, in learning how to use the guide words found on the top of each page, and how to fit the correct dictionary definition into the context where he found the unknown word.

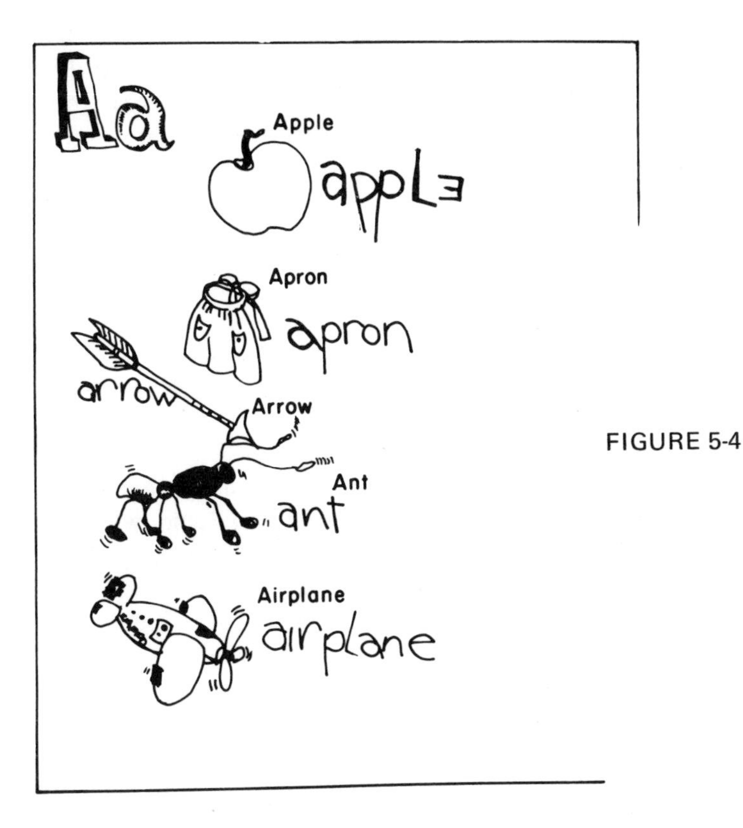

FIGURE 5-4

This really is very difficult since sometimes none of the words exactly fit the requirements of the unknown word.

Usually the teacher in a reading improvement program should show the child how to use a dictionary at his instructional grade level when he really needs to find the meaning of an unknown word which he cannot find by using any other word recognition technique. Such motivated life-like practice gives a disabled reader a real reason to learn how to use the dictionary and he is therefore apt to be more interested in learning this skill when he has a real need.

Of course, the teacher also can construct worksheets which give the child some practice in using the dictionary. A good source of suggestions in helping the teacher construct such worksheets are a basal reader teacher's manual or a basal reader workbook at the proper instructional grade level. However, such worksheets generally are not as valuable in teaching dictionary usage as actual practice when a child looks up the meaning of a word that he really wants to know. However, such worksheets can be individually tailored to the child's special interests to help him want to learn dictionary usage. The following is an example of a teacher-made worksheet to teach the use of guide words in a simplified dictionary:

____

Name

1. On what page are the guide words "lovebird" and "loyalty?"
2. Look up the word home. What are the two guide words on this page?
3. What are the two guide words on page 663?
4. On what page do you find the guide words "root" and "rosy?"
5. Look up the word nickel. What are the two guide words on this page?
6. What are the two guide words on page 488?
7. What are the two guide words on page 354?
8. Look up the word face. What are the two guide words on that page?
9. Look up the word crown. What are the two guide words on that page?
10. On what page are the guide words "devote" and "dialect?"[2]

The following are several simplified dictionaries which can be used in a reading improvement program:

Webster's New Elementary Dictionary. American Book Company, 300 Pike Street, Cincinnati, Ohio 45202.

Webster's New Practical School Dictionary. American Book Company, 300 Pike Street, Cincinnati, Ohio 45202.

Webster's New Student Dictionary. American Book Company, 300 Pike Street, Cincinnati, Ohio 45202.

A thesaurus also can be used to teach dictionary skills. A thesaurus lists many synonyms of words which have the same meaning as the word which the child looks up. A thesaurus can be of value to a child with an intermediate-grade instructional reading

---

[2]*Webster's New Practical School Dictionary.* New York: American Book Company, 1964.

level. The following is an example of a thesaurus for use at this level:

> Greet, W. Cabell, William A. Jenkins, and Andrew Schiller. *In Other Words.* Scott, Foresman and Company, Glenview, Illinois, 60025, 1969.

Glossary usage requires many of the same skills that effective dictionary usage does. Effective glossary usage requires that a child know alphabetical sequence, phonetic analysis, and to an extent the ability to use a word in context. However, usually there is only one definition of the word in a glossary, and the definition fits into the context where it is needed. Glossary usage can best be taught by motivated practice and looking the word up when the child needs it in his own reading. Of course, the teacher also can construct worksheets in glossary usage, but they are not as effective as purposeful practice.

SUMMARY

This chapter illustrated how any reading improvement program must correct the specific word recognition difficulties that a disabled reader has. It gave many suggestions on how to teach the word recognition techniques of word form clues, phonetic analysis, structural analysis, picture and context clues, and dictionary usage. The chapter also listed materials to correct difficulties in these word recognition skills.

Word form clues are a word recognition skill in which a reader recognizes a word by its total shape, form, or configuration. A difficulty in recognizing the 220 service words on the Dolch Basic Sight Word Test is fairly common among disabled readers. To build a child's stock of sight words the Fernald Tracing Method, the language-experience approach, several games, and word cards can be used. It is important for a disabled reader to see his progress in learning these sight words in some concrete way.

Phonetic analysis is the association of sound (phoneme) and symbol (grapheme). Analytic phonetic analysis usually is considered to be the best type of phonetic analysis, and most reading specialists recommend using the inductive or discovery method of teaching phonetic analysis. A disabled reader should receive systematic instruction only in the areas of phonetic analysis in which he was found to be weak. Auditory discrimination must be developed first for the disabled readers who are very weak in phonetic analysis. Rhyming games, objects beginning with the same sounds, a sensitizing experience, and some records can be used to promote auditory discrimination. The teacher can use the basal reader manuals of any good reading series, basal reader workbooks, phonics materials, teacher-made worksheets, and phonic games to develop a disabled reader's ability in phonetic analysis.

Structural analysis involves the use of base words, prefixes and suffixes, syllabication, accent, and compound words to help a reader get the pronunciation and meaning of words. Structural analysis rules should be taught in an inductive or discovery method. Readiness for syllabication is begun at the first reader level with a child's tapping out or clapping the number of syllables he hears in a list of words the teacher pronounces for him. Many useful suggestions for teaching structural analysis skills are available in the basal reader teacher's manuals. Other sources of practice materials are found in basal reader workbook pages, teacher-made worksheets, and games. The Fernald Tracing Method can be used in teaching syllabication.

Picture clues involve the use of a picture to get the meaning of an unknown word on the same page or on a nearby page. The teacher must show the disabled reader how to use a picture in this way. Context clues are used when a reader gets the meaning of an unknown word from how it is used in the sentence or paragraph in which it is found. To correct difficulties in the use of context clues, the teacher can use the basal reader manuals, pages from the basal reader workbooks, or construct her own worksheets. Wide reading of easy material can also develop a child's ability to use context clues.

Dictionary usage should be taught to many older, mildly disabled readers. Dictionary readiness can take the form of alphabetizing several words or using a picture dicitonary or pictionary. Actual instruction in dictionary usage can be begun at the later third-grade reading level. The teacher can find guidance in teaching this skill from the teacher's edition of a simplified dictionary. Motivated life-like practice gives a disabled reader a real reason to learn dictionary usage. Teacher-made worksheets also can be of help in teaching dictionary usage. Glossary usage requires most of the same skills of dictionary usage.

REFERENCES

Bond, Guy L. and Miles A. Tinker. *Reading Difficulties: Their Diagnosis and Correction.* New York: Appleton-Century-Crofts, 1967. Chapter 12.

Carter, Homer L. J. and Dorothy J. McGinnis. *Diagnosis and Treatment of the Disabled Reader.* New York: The Macmillan Company, 1970. Chapter 11.

Harris, Albert J. *How to Increase Reading Ability.* New York: David McKay Company, Incorporated, 1970. Chapter 13.

Heilman, Arthur W. *Principles and Practices of Teaching Reading.* Columbus, Ohio: Charles E. Merrill Publishing Company, 1967. Chapter 9.

Miller, Wilma H. *The First R: Elementary Reading Today.* New York: Holt, Rinehart and Winston, Incorporated, 1972. Chapter 11.

Tinker, Miles A. and Constance M. McCullough. *Teaching Elementary Reading.* New York: Appleton-Century-Crofts, Incorporated, 1968. Chapter 8.

6

Correcting Comprehension Difficulties

Chapter 5 discussed how to correct difficulties in the various word recognition techniques. As Chapter 1 indicated, word recognition skills come before comprehension abilities in the reading process. Therefore, a child must have good recognition techniques before he is able to understand what he is reading. However, a few disabled readers have adequate word recognition skills but are still unable to effectively understand what they are reading.

This chapter explains vocabulary development and its relation to reading comprehension, and describes comprehension in terms of the following levels: the literal or factual level, the higher-type or inferential level, critical reading, and creative or integrative reading. The chapter also illustrates some ways to correct comprehension difficulties at these various levels and provides a list of materials at various instructional reading levels to correct these difficulties.

Correcting Difficulties in Vocabulary Development

Effective comprehension at any level depends upon good word recognition techniques and a good meaning vocabulary. A reader cannot understand what he is reading effectively if he meets too many unknown words in his reading. A meaningful vocabulary mainly is developed when a reader has many kinds of experiences.

Therefore, the culturally disadvantaged child often has a limited vocabulary due to a lack of worthwhile experiences in the home.

The teacher can discover if a disabled reader has a limited meaning vocabulary in a number of ways. She can examine the vocabulary or word meaning subtest on either a standardized survey or achievement test. She also can make up an informal vocabulary test which she can include as part of the individual reading inventory. The words on this test can be taken from those found in a basal reader at the appropriate instructional reading level. The teacher also can observe and listen to the child while he is speaking to notice informally the extent and quality of his vocabulary. The teacher may notice that the disadvantaged child or the slow-learning child has a restricted vocabulary with many imprecise words.

When the teacher has found that a child has a limited vocabulary, she can help him overcome this deficiency in a number of ways. For a child in the elementary school, first-hand or direct experiences certainly are the best way to build vocabulary. Such direct experiences can take the form of interesting trips to places in the neighborhood near the school, such as the grocery store, the bakery, or the dairy. To get the most in vocabulary development from these trips, the teacher can talk about what kinds of things the children will see when they do take the field trip, can point out the interesting objects while they are on the trip, and can let the children use the newly learned vocabulary words back in the schoolroom in talking and writing activities. Other kinds of direct experiences are handling concrete objects, construction activities, and role playing.

Second-hand or vicarious experiences also are good for developing vocabulary in any disabled reader in the elementary school. They are not generally as good as direct experiences, but sometimes they can be a valuable substitute for direct experiences which a child might otherwise not be able to have. Some examples of vicarious experiences are looking at films and film strips, looking at pictures, listening to records, and reading easy, interesting materials. Wide reading of such material probably is one of the better ways to develop vocabulary since a child can learn the meanings of many words by using context clues in this way. However, if he is to get the most help from the use of context clues, the material should be easy enough to insure that there will not be too many unknown words in it. If a child reads a number of easy science textbooks, it is obvious that he will learn some new vocabulary words just by this reading.

The teacher also can present words that a child commonly needs to know when he is reading. Several reading specialists have surveyed reading materials at the elementary level and have made up some vocabulary lists of commonly used words in reading which every child eventually should learn. Some of these word lists are as follows:

B.R. Buckingham and E.W. Dolch. *A Combined Word List.* Boston: Ginn and Company, Waltham, Massachusetts 02154.

Edgar Dale. *The Dale List of 3,000 Words.* Printed in Edgar Dale and Jeanne S. Chall, "A Formula for Predicting Readability," *Educational Research Bulletin,* Ohio State University, 27, (January 21, 1948, and February 18, 1948), pp. 11-20, 28, and 37-54.

E.L. Thorndike and Irving Lorge. *The Teacher's Word Book of 30,000 Words.* New York: Teachers College Press, Columbia University, 525 West 120th Street, New York 10027.

The study of prefixes and its relation to vocabulary development was explained in detail in Chapter 5. The study of prefixes can be of help to some brighter, older disabled readers who are interested in it. Dictionary usage and its relation to the development of word meanings also was explained in detail in Chapter 5. There also are some materials for vocabulary development which can be helpful mainly for older disabled readers. Some of these materials are as follows:

Lee C. Deighton. *Vocabulary Development.* The Macmillan Reading Spectrum. New York: The Macmillan Company, 866 Third Avenue, New York 10022.

Word Clues. Huntington, New York: Educational Developmental Laboratories. 11743

Correcting Difficulties in Literal Comprehension

As Chapter 1 described, comprehension of what is read first depends on satisfactory eye movements and a good knowledge of the different word recognition techniques. Most of the modern reading approaches emphasize literal comprehension from the beginning stages of reading instruction. Literal comprehension probably receives the most stress in the basal reader, language-experience, and individualized reading approaches. It often receives less stress in any formal phonics program and in the linguistic approaches as will be illustrated in Chapter 8.

Literal or factual comprehension is a low level of understanding and really consists of two separate levels. The lowest level of literal comprehension is reproduction, in which a child just reproduces the words of the author in answering a question. A higher level or literal comprehension is called translation in which the child translates or paraphrases the author's words in answering questions but does not think in a real way about his answers before giving them. The following are some examples of literal comprehension questions on the second grade instructional reading level:

Where had Red and Rusty lived?

How long had Rusty lived there?

What town was Rusty born in?

What color was Janet's hair?

What did Rusty's grandfather want to trade Red for?[1]

Literal comprehension should receive much stress in the primary grades and receive less stress in the intermediate grades. As a child progresses in reading, he should be able to answer more higher-type comprehension questions. If a child has good word recognition skills, he normally will not have too much difficulty with literal comprehension. Therefore, the reading teacher probably will not see very many disabled readers with good word recognition skills who have difficulty with literal comprehension.

In discovering if a child has difficulty with literal comprehension, there are a number of sources which a teacher can use. To some extent she can determine this from using the results of a standardized survey or diagnostic reading test. However, the teacher must examine the kinds of comprehension questions on the test to determine if they are mainly literal questions. She can also use an oral reading test to discover this difficulty since these tests stress factual comprehension. Several oral reading tests were discussed in Chapter 3. She also can use the comprehension questions on the graded oral reading paragraphs of the individual reading inventory. Of course, she should examine only the questions dealing with factual comprehension. The teacher also can

[1]Mabel O'Donnell, *All Through the Year.* New York: Harper and Row, Publishers, 1966, pp. 36-41.

notice the way the disabled reader is able to answer literal comprehension questions about basal reader stories or tradebooks on his appropriate reading level.

If a disabled reader has difficulty with factual comprehension, there are a number of ways the teacher can use to correct this difficulty. Probably the best source of suggestions for the teacher to use in working with a disabled reader are the literal comprehension questions provided in the teacher's manual of the appropriate basal reader. Of course, the child should always read from basal readers on his own instructional grade level, and the teacher should always be sure that he is reading for meaning. She can do this by being sure that he can answer the comprehension questions she asks him while he is reading a story in a basal reader. Of course, the teacher can make up her own literal comprehension questions for use with any basal reader story.

The teacher also can use language-experience stories or tradebooks to teach or to give practice on literal comprehension skills. In such a case the child probably would read a language-experience story or tradebook silently, and the teacher then asks him a number of literal comprehension questions to test his understanding of it. It is obvious that the tradebooks that are used for this purpose should always be on the disabled reader's independent or free reading level and usually should be of interest to him.

Some of the basal reader workbook pages on the appropriate instructional reading level also can be used for practice in literal comprehension. However, such pages probably are of much help if the disabled reader's instructional reading level is on a primary-grade reading level since basal reader workbooks at the intermediate-grade level usually emphasize higher-type comprehension. Of course, only the workbook pages dealing with factual comprehension should be used if the child has been found to have difficulty in this area.

The teacher can prepare worksheets which would be of help in developing literal comprehension ability. Such a worksheet could have a story typed on the top half of a sheet of paper with a primary typewriter or a regular typewriter depending upon the child's age and reading level. Such a story could be a language-experience story which the child had dictated to the teacher earlier or could be a story on the child's instructional or independent reading levels which the teacher has made up specifically to capitalize on the child's particular interest. As an example, if a disabled reader were interested in model cars, the teacher could make up a story about model cars on his reading grade level. On the bottom half of the sheet the teacher can write a number of literal comprehension questions about the story which the child can answer either orally or in writing depending upon his age and ability. Capitalizing on his own interests can motivate him to improve his comprehension ability.

Directions calling for literal comprehension also can help to improve ability in this area. Such directions are typed or printed on a strip of oaktag or paper as in Figure 6-1, and the disabled reader is to read and carry out the direction.

Go to the door and open it.

FIGURE 6-1

The directions can involve physical movement or can involve something which is pleasant for the child as the following examples show:

> Go to my desk over in the corner of the room. You can have what is in the right-hand drawer.
>
> You can open the window of this room.
>
> You can get the picture that is on my desk and put it anywhere on the bulletin board that you want to.
>
> Go to the door and open it.
>
> Write your name on this piece of paper for me.

Sometimes difficulty in literal comprehension results when a child reads in a word-by-word way. This often results because he has been allowed to read orally in this way in the early primary grades. Difficulty in understanding can result because the child is paying too much attention to each word and cannot therefore sense the relation between the words in the sentence to get the idea of the whole sentence. Word-by-word reading can be overcome by letting the child do much reading on very easy interesting material. Such practice helps him to develop reading fluency and to concentrate on the thoughts or ideas in each sentence instead of on the individual word in each sentence.

Word-by-word reading also can be corrected by teaching the child reading on the later primary or intermediate-grade reading level to read in thought units or groups of several words at one time or fixation. This can be done by using flash cards made of oaktag or cardboard with a thought unit or phrase printed on it, as shown in Figure 6-2.

FIGURE 6-2

A tachistoscope flashes phrases on the screen at certain time intervals and can be used to correct word-by-word reading. A tachistoscope is a reading machine which is used to improve visual perception and flashes words or phrases on a screen at speeds of one-tenth of a second to one-hundredth of a second. A tachistoscope can be purchased from the following companies:

Educational Developmental Laboratories, Huntington, New York 11743.

Keystone View Company, Meadville, Pennsylvania 16335.

There also are special books and workbooks available which are designed to develop literal comprehension ability. Most of these can develop both literal and higher-type comprehension, so the teacher must choose the appropriate exercises from the following list of materials:

Clarence Stone and Charles Grover, et. al. *New Practice Readers,* Webster Division, McGraw-Hill Book Company, Manchester Road, Manchester, Missouri 63011.

Richard A. Boning. *Specific Skills Series.* Barnell Loft, Ltd., 111 South Centre Avenue, Rockville Centre, New York 11570.

New Reading Skill Builder Series, Reader's Digest Services, Incorporated, Pleasantville, New York 10570.

New Reading Skilltext Series. Charles E. Merrill Company, 1300 Alum Creek Drive, Columbus, Ohio 43216.

There is a game to help develop phrase perception and it is Sight Phrase Cards, The Garrard Press, Champaign, Illinois 61820.

Correcting Difficulties in Higher-Type Comprehension

Higher-type or inferential comprehension first depends on skill in word recognition, but this is a high level of understanding in which a reader must think for himself in some way before he answers the questions which are asked. Higher-type comprehension consists of the skills of predicting outcomes, drawing conclusions and generalizations, sensing the author's mood and purpose, interpreting what is read, and reading between the lines. Inferential comprehension should receive stress from the beginning stages of reading when a child in first grade is asked to think about what he has read. Higher-type comprehension illustrates the statement that: "Reading is a thinking process."

Higher-type comprehension usually receives more stress in the intermediate grades and should receive great stress at the secondary level. Higher-type comprehension depends upon a child's ability to do abstract thinking. Therefore, many slow-learning children will have difficulty with it. However, much of the time a child does not think inferentially because no one has asked him questions which call for this type of thought. Without higher-type comprehension, a child who can pronounce the words adequately is called a "word-caller" or "verbalizer." Several examples of higher-type comprehension questions are as follows:

Why is it difficult for a dog to live in the city instead of in the country?

Can you think why Red likes Janet?

Why do you think there was no room in the city for a dog as big as Red?

Why do you think a cat might be a better pet for Rusty to have in the city?

Do you think Rusty's grandparents really like Red?[2]

Some disabled readers who have good word recognition techniques do have some difficulty with higher-type comprehension. This can be due to a child's limited intellectual development. It also can result from inadequate experiences as is sometimes found in a culturally disadvantaged child. A limited

---

[2]Mabel O'Donnell. *All Through the Year.* New York: Harper and Row, Publishers, 1966, pp. 36-41.

vocabulary and a lack of concepts also can cause difficulty with higher-type comprehension.

Difficulties with higher-type comprehension can be located by the teacher in several different ways as Chapter III illustrated. Most of the standardized survey and diagnostic reading tests contain some higher-type comprehension questions. The oral reading tests are of little value in this area since they mainly call for factual responses. The higher-type comprehension questions on the graded oral reading paragraphs in the individual reading inventory are of great value in determining difficulties in this area. Informal observation of the child as he answers higher-type comprehension questions which the teacher asks him after he has read a basal reader story or a tradebook also can give her clues to possible difficulties.

One very good source of suggestions for inferential comprehension questions is the teacher's manual of the basal reader at the appropriate instructional grade level. If a child has difficulty with higher-type comprehension, many worthwhile questions should be asked him while he is reading a basal reader story. Of course, the teacher also can formulate her own inferential comprehension questions for any of the stories in the basal reader at the appropriate grade level.

Appropriate pages from a basal reader workbook can be used to improve inferential comprehension. Only those workbook pages dealing directly with inferential comprehension should be used, and they should always be on the child's instructional reading level.

The teacher can construct her own worksheets to teach and reinforce higher-type comprehension. She can use a dictated experience story or a story which she has made up that effectively will capitalize on the child's special interests. She then can type this story with a primary typewriter or a regular typewriter depending on the child's age on the top half of a sheet of paper and type inferential questions on the bottom half of the sheet. The child can then answer these questions either orally or in writing depending upon his age and ability. Obviously, the use of his experiences or special interests will greatly motivate him to improve his higher-type comprehension skills.

There are a number of special materials in the form of reading laboratories, workbooks, and games which can be used either to teach or reinforce higher-type comprehension skills. Any of these materials should be on the disabled reader's instructional level and should interest him as much as possible. None of these materials should be used as the only approach in this area. They should be used as one approach to teach inferential comprehension skills, and they should be used for only part of any corrective or remedial reading session. The following is a list of materials to develop higher-type comprehension for disabled readers:

Reading for Meaning. J. B. Lippincott Company, East Washington Square, Philadelphia, Pennsylvania 19105.

The Reading Skill Builders. Reader's Digest Services, Incorporated, Pleasantville, New York 10570.

Reading for Understanding, Junior Edition. Science Research Associates, 259 East Erie Street, Chicago, Illinois 60611.

Reading Laboratory Series, 1a, 1b, 1c, 2a, 2b, and 2c. Science Research Associates, 250 East Erie Street, Chicago, Illinois 60611.

The Macmillan Reading Spectrum. The Macmillan Company, 866 Third Avenue, New York 10022.

Nila Banton Smith. *Be A Better Reader.* Prentice-Hall Incorporated, Englewood Cliffs, New Jersey 07632.

Eleanor M. Johnson. *Diagnostic Reading Workbooks.* Charles E. Merrill Books, Incorporated, 1300 Alum Creek Drive, Columbus, Ohio 43216.

U.W. Leavell, et al. *New Goals in Reading.* Steck-Vaughn Company, P. O. Box 2028, Austin, Texas 78767.

Correcting Difficulties in Critical Reading

Critical reading can be defined as evaluating or judging what is read in terms of criteria which the reader has formed from his past experiences. As Chapter I described critical reading is a high level of the reading process. Therefore, most disabled readers do not need specific instruction in this area unless they are mildly disabled older readers who are in the intermediate grades or in junior high school. The vast majority of the disabled readers whom the teacher meets have difficulty with either word recognition techniques or comprehension ability. Since ability in critical reading first depends upon ability in word recognition and comprehension, most disabled readers do not read well enough to need special instruction in critical reading.

However, critical reading ability can be developed to a small extent as early as the reading readiness level when a child is asked to interpret a picture critically or asked to tell the difference between fact and fantasy. It can be further extended at the first reader instructional level and certainly should receive more emphasis when a child is reading on the intermediate-grade instructional reading level. At this level critical questions ask the child to judge the accuracy or truthfulness of what they read, to tell the difference between fact and fiction, and to understand the various propaganda techniques such as testimonials, the halo effect, the band wagon technique, cardstacking, and glittering generalities. These propaganda techniques attempt to influence a reader in subtle ways without their realizing that any one is attempting to influence him.

It is necessary that any mature reader become as critical a reader as possible. Therefore, it is important for the teacher to put some stress on critical reading for older, mildly disabled readers as one aspect of comprehension. The following are some questions which call for critical answers on the sixth-grade instructional reading level:

> This story states that no plants can live on lava rock. How can you prove that this is true?
>
> How can you prove the truthfulness of the following statement: But the wind was also loaded with invisible clouds of living things too tiny to see?
>
> How can you prove the accuracy of the following statement: On their feathers and bills were seeds from the thick matting of plants where they had nested. These new seeds sprouted and grew on the island.[3]

At the present time there is no standardized test except a test in an experimental form which makes any attempt to judge a child's ability in critical reading. Therefore, the teacher can discover weaknesses in this area by asking the disabled reader questions calling for critical responses after he has read a basal reader story or a tradebook on his level. If he often cannot answer critical questions, he probably needs some motivated practice in this area. It should again be emphasized that instruction in critical

---

[3]Eldonna L. Evertts and Byron H. VanRoekel. *Seven Seas.* New York: Harper and Row, Publishers, 1966, pp. 145-161.

reading should be left until the child has sufficient ability in word recognition and comprehension to be able to understand what he is reading.

Once the difficulty has been discovered, the teacher can correct it in several ways. She can simply ask the child to answer critical questions about the various basal reader stories or trade-books which he has read on his own reading level. If a child is never asked a question that calls for a critical answer, he never will give a critical answer. If several children who have this difficulty and who read on about the same instructional grade level are grouped, the group answers can stimulate critical thinking and inquiry in the other group members. This type of activity mainly uses basal reader stories and is called a directed reading activity.

Some basal reader workbooks may contain pages which partially are devoted to the development of critical reading. Often these questions are found on a page with higher-type comprehension questions instead of on a page by themselves. Only the workbook pages dealing with this skill on the disabled reader's instructional reading level should be used. Often such workbooks are more likely to be found on the intermediate-grade reading level where critical reading receives more emphasis.

The teacher can also construct her own worksheets to develop ability in critical reading. She can type a story with a primary typewriter or a regular typewriter on the top half of a sheet of paper, and make up some questions calling for critical responses on the bottom half of the sheet. The disabled reader can then answer these questions calling for critical responses in writing.

The teacher also can pose several questions to be researched by a disabled reader from subject matter textbooks in the areas of social studies and science on his instructional or independent reading level. The child should use at least two textbooks to find the answer to the same question. This shows him how important it is to read critically without accepting as the truth every statement which is found in a textbook.

Newspapers can be used to develop critical reading ability at the upper intermediate instructional grade level. A child can be taught to read various newspaper articles while evaluating their accuracy. However, a child must have an instructional reading level at about the sixth-grade level to succeed in this kind of activity since most newspapers are written on this level. However, newspapers can be a good motivation for many older disabled readers.

There are very few materials available which may help to develop critical reading ability. The following material is more for older disabled readers:

> William A. McCall and Edwin A. Smith. *Test Lessons in Reading-Reasoning.* New York: Teachers College Press, Columbia University, 525 West 120th Street, New York 10017.

Correcting Difficulties in Creative Reading

Chapter 1 illustrated that the highest level of the reading process is creative reading or the applying of what is read to the reader's own life for problem-solving. Creative reading is the ultimate goal of all reading instruction.

It is obvious that most disabled readers have difficulty with the lower levels of reading such as word recognition or comprehension. However, as soon as a child has achieved a little proficiency in these areas, the teacher can give him many opportunities to read creatively or to apply what he reads to his own life in some way. Creative reading can be used as early as the first-grade instructional reading level when a child makes something as the result of reading about how to do it. Bibliotherapy or the solving of a personal problem through reading about someone who had a similar problem also is reading creatively.

The following are some ways a child can read creatively at the third-grade instructional reading level:

> Try to make an Indian peacepipe like the one Mark bought.
> Write a story about the Indians who live in the North Woods.
> Draw a map showing how Mark and Janet got from the North Woods to their house in Redwood City.
> Draw a map of the state that you live in.[4]

Of course, there are no standardized reading tests which measure a child's ability to read creatively. This must be judged by the teacher after she has the child read a basal reader story or a tradebook which calls for him to do something or to make something after reading about it. Bibliotherapy can change a

[4] Mabel O'Donnell. *From Faraway Places.* New York: Harper and Row, Publishers, 1966, pp. 9-35.

child's attitude or behavior in some way, and this must be judged by the teacher through observation.

In correcting difficulties in this area, the teacher must choose materials from basal readers, tradebooks, or textbooks on the appropriate reading level and then help the child to apply the reading for problem-solving in some way. The child must be able to comprehend the material and carry out the directions found in it.

The teacher also can construct typed directions on a sheet of paper which the child can easily read and use for problem-solving. Such directions might capitalize on the child's special interests such as putting together a model farm or a model city. The directions must be easy for the child to read and clear enough for him to easily carry out. Obviously, materials also must be available for carrying out the directions on the worksheets.

SUMMARY

This chapter discussed vocabulary development and its relation to reading comprehension. To develop vocabulary, first-hand or direct experiences certainly are the most valuable. However, second-hand or vicarious experiences can be a valuable substitute for direct experiences. Wide reading also is a very good way to develop vocabulary by using context clues.

Literal comprehension is a low level of understanding and consists of reproduction and translation. It should receive some stress in the primary grades. The basal reader teacher's manual on the appropriate reading level and pages from the basal reader workbooks can be useful in improving literal comprehension. Teacher-prepared worksheets with a story and literal comprehension questions also can be of help in this area. Directions calling for literal comprehension can provide motivation. The chapter discussed word-by-word reading and showed its relation to literal comprehension. Materials were listed for developing ability in this area.

Higher-type comprehension is a high level of understanding in which a reader thinks for himself before he answers the questions which are asked. The teacher's manual of a basal reader at the appropriate instructional grade level or appropriate pages from a basal reader workbook can be used to improve higher-type comprehension. The teacher can prepare her own worksheets with a story and higher-type comprehension questions on it to develop ability in this area. The chapter also listed a number of special materials to teach or reinforce higher-type comprehension skills.

Critical reading is evaluating what is read in terms of criteria that the reader has formed from his past experiences. It is a high level of the reading process. The teacher can ask the child critical questions about basal reader stories or tradebooks which he has read. The directed reading activity with several children can be of help in this area. Basal reader workbook pages or teacher-prepared worksheets also can help to develop a child's critical reading ability. Unit teaching and the use of newspapers also can develop critical reading ability.

Creative reading is the applying of what is read to the reader's own life for problem-solving and is the highest level of the reading process. The child can read materials and then apply what he has read by making or constructing something or by solving a personal problem which he has.

REFERENCES

Bond, Guy L. and Miles A. Tinker. *Reading Difficulties: Their Diagnosis and Correction.* New York: Appleton-Century-Crofts, Incorporated, 1967. Chapter 11.

Carter, Homer L. J. and Dorothy J. McGinnis. *Diagnosis and Treatment of the Disabled Reader.* New York: The Macmillan Company, 1970. Chapter 13.

Dechant, Emerald V. *Improving the Teaching of Reading.* Englewood Cliffs, New Jersey: Prentice-Hall, Incorporated, 1970. Chapter 13.

Harris, Albert J. *How to Increase Reading Ability.* New York: David McKay Company, Incorporated, 1970. Chapters 15 and 16.

Miller, Wilma H. *The First R: Elementary Reading Today.* New York: Holt, Rinehart and Winston, Incorporated, 1972. Chapter 13.

Tinker, Miles A. and Constance M. McCullough. *Teaching Elementary Reading.* New York: Appleton-Century-Crofts, Incorporated, 1968. Chapter 9.

7

Meeting the Reading Needs of Individuals

Slow-learning children, reluctant readers, and culturally disadvantaged children are discussed in this chapter. The chapter describes the characteristics of a typical slow-learning child and outlines methods and materials which can be used to help him to improve his reading in the elementary classroom. The able reluctant reader also is discussed and the best methods and materials to use to motivate him to use his reading skills effectively are outlined. The chapter also discusses the characteristics of a culturally disadvantaged child and illustrates the most effective methods and materials to use with him in an elementary classroom. A positive approach is stressed in this chapter which builds upon the strengths of each child and shows the best ways to correct his weaknesses.

Characteristics of the Slow-Learning Child

There are a number of criteria which can be used to determine if a child in an elementary classroom really is a slow-learning child. Obviously, the most important and widely-used characteristic is the child's rate of learning or intelligence quotient as discovered from a group or an individual intelligence test as was described in Chapter 3. The individual intelligence test gives an intelligence quotient which is the more accurate, but even this kind of test can underestimate a slow-learning child's actual intellectual ability. The slow-learning child usually has an intelligence quotient of from 70 to 90.

The teacher can use a number of other characteristics to determine if a child really is a slow-learner. If she teaches him something very thoroughly and he does not seem to learn it as easily and quickly as most of the other children in the classroom, he may be a slow-learning child. However, this is not always completely accurate since the child may not learn well because of other reasons such as poor motivation, chronic illnesses, or emotional maladjustment. Obviously, slow-learning children achieve in all school learnings at a rate that is much slower than most of the other children. Often they do not show much curiosity or interest in school and appear to be passive and withdrawn especially if they are asked to do work in school which they really cannot do. Slow-learning children do better in school with work which requires concrete thinking since they usually have trouble in thinking at an abstract level. Therefore, in reading they often have difficulty with higher-type comprehension and critical reading while they can do much better with factual comprehension.

As was discussed in Chapter 2, any slow-learning child usually needs an extended reading readiness period in school if he is going to be able to learn to read well. A slow-learning child just does not have the mental age necessary for success in beginning reading at the chronological age of six or seven. Most slow-learning children cannot do well with reading instruction until they have reached a chronological age of eight. Such an extended reading readiness period probably may not be practical for such children, but at least they should have one semester of readiness development in first grade.

A Program for Slow-Learning Children in the Primary Grades

The extended reading readiness period and beginning reading activities gradually can blend together for slow-learning children so that it is difficult to tell when one ends and the other begins. The *Frostig Program for the Development of Visual Perception* can be of help for many slow-learning children since they often are weak in visual perception.[1] This program consists of a test to measure a child's perceptual quotient, a series of physical exercises to enhance motor coordination, and a series of workbooks to teach visual perception skills in the areas of figure-ground perception, perceptual constancy, perception of position in space, visual-motor coordination, and perception of spatial relationships.

The language-experience approach can also be used to develop a slow-learning child's reading readiness as well as to help him begin a program of reading instruction. This approach is described in detail in Chapter 8, but it uses child-dictated and child-written experience stories and group-dictated experience charts. In the early stages of its use, the teacher types the child-dictated experience stories using a primary typewriter, and the child illustrates his stories or attaches a photograph of himself doing what is written about him in the stories. The child and teacher then can "read" the stories back together, and the child learns words by sight from the stories.

For slow-learning children in the primary grades, a reading program which involves much concrete, meaningful repetition of the reading skills probably is of the most value. Such children need much repetition especially of the various word recognition skills. Such a reading program can be either a basal reader approach or a formal phonics program, both of which are described in Chapter 8. In either type of reading program the rate of instruction should, of course, be slow and deliberate. There is no point in "covering" the book if the child gets nothing from it. It is much better to present reading instruction so slowly that the slow-learning child always can experience success with it since a poor self-concept is difficult to correct once the child has it. Usually a slow-learning child should meet with his basal reader group or phonics group about four days a week in the primary grades.

A supplementary phonics program often can be of value for those slow-learning children who are learning to read by a basal reader approach and who have good auditory discrimination (the ability to hear likenesses and differences in sounds.) Several supplementary phonics programs which can be recommended with slow-learning children are the *Phonovisual Method,* the *Hegge-*

---

[1]Marianne Frostig and David Horne, *The Frostig Program for the Development of Visual Perception.* Chicago: Follett Publishing Company, 1964.

Kirk-Kirk Remedial Reading Drills, Breaking the Sound Barrier, and *Reading with Phonics.*[2] However, the teacher should try to keep these programs as practical and meaningful as possible if slow-learning children are to gain much from them.

A kinesthetic or VAKT Method can be useful with some slow-learning children since it uses all of their senses in learning to recognize a word. As was described in Chapter 4, it probably is better to use the Fernald Tracing Method rather than to use the Gillingham-Stillman Method since the Fernald Method uses the saying and tracing of syllables rather than of isolated sounds.

Self-instructional programmed materials in the form of workbooks or teaching machines can be useful to reinforce some reading skills, probably especially the word recognition skills. Programmed materials let slow-learning children have meaningful repetition, experience immediate success, learn on a concrete level, and use material which has been divided into small logical units. Some useful programmed materials are *Programmed Reading, Reading in High Gear,* and *Lift Off to Reading.*[3]

The individualized reading plan also can be helpful in the reading instruction of slow-learning children in the primary grades. The individualized reading plan is described in Chapter 8. This plan gives children the opportunity to reinforce their reading skills using self-selected materials such as simple tradebooks, simple subject matter textbooks, and easy children's magazines and newspapers. With slow-learning children, the individualized reading plan mainly can be used to motivate reading rather than to teach reading skills. Such children very much enjoy the one-to-one relationship they have with their teacher in the individual reading conference. The teacher should probably give slow-learning children considerable help in choosing materials that they can easily read since they always should experience success in independent

---

[2]See: Lucille D. Schoolfield and Josephine B. Timberlake, *Phonovisual Method.* Washington, D. C.: Phonovisual Products, 1944; T. Hegge, Samuel Kirk, and Winifred Kirk, *Remedial Reading Drills.* Ann Arbor, Michigan: George Wahr, Publisher, 1955; Sister Mary Caroline, *Breaking the Sound Barrier.* New York: The Macmillan Company, 1960; Julie Hay and Charles E. Wingo, *Reading with Phonics.* Philadelphia: J. B. Lippincott Company, 1967.

[3]See: Cynthia Dee Buchanan, *Sullivan Programmed Reading.* St. Louis: Webster Division, McGraw-Hill Book Company, 1963; Myron Woolman, *Reading in High Gear,* Chicago: Science Research Associates, 1965; Myron Woolman, *Lift Off to Reading.* Chicago: Science Research Associates, 1966.

reading. Individualized reading can be used about one day a week with slow-learning children in the primary grades.

Slow-learning children need to see their progress in reading in some concrete way. They need much extrinsic or outside motivation and rewards in the form of progress charts, gold stars, or some other concrete way. They always must experience success with reading for if they become discouraged with their lack of progress, they will give up trying. However, a slow-learning child in the primary grades can experience success with reading if his reading expectancy level is kept clearly in mind by his teacher.

A Program for Slow-Learning Children in the Intermediate Grades

The basal reader approach probably is a good way of extending the word recognition and comprehension skills of slow-learning children in the intermediate grades. Of course, the basal reader approach should continue from the point at which it stopped when the child completed third grade. If he enters fourth-grade reading on a beginning second-grade level, obviously the reading instruction should begin at that point. It may be wise to continue the same basal reader series which was used in the primary grades since the various word recognition and comprehension skills then will be presented in a sequential developmental manner.

The basal reader materials should be presented in a very slow and thorough way to insure that each reading skill almost is overlearned. There is no value in "covering" a basal reader if the child does not thoroughly and completely learn all of the word recognition and comprehension skills which are presented in that reader. A slow-learning child in the intermediate grades can make good progress in reading if he uses basal readers on his instructional reading level, and if the reading skills are presented in a careful thorough way.

Some slow-learning children in the intermediate grades who have good auditory discrimination may profit from a formal phonics program if they are weak in phonetic analysis skills by the time they reach the intermediate grades. This should not happen if phonetic analysis skills were presented to them carefully in the later primary grades and each one was mastered. However, several phonics programs can be recommended for slow learners in the intermediate grades. They are the Hegge-Kirk-Kirk *Remedial Reading Drills,* the *Lippincott Basic Reading Program,* and *Phonetic Keys to Reading.*[4] As in the primary grades, the teacher must be very careful that a formal phonics program does not become a rote memorization of phonics rules.

The unit plan often can be very effective in a reading program with slow-learning children in the intermediate grades. The unit plan can easily be used in the areas of social studies, science, or health. The unit either can involve the entire class, an intellectually mixed group of children, or a group of slow-learning children. A topic for the unit is chosen, and the teacher then helps each child to read about some part of the unit from reading materials which are on his independent or free reading level. For an intermediate-grade slow-learning child, the independent reading level probably will be on the first or second grade reading level. Unit reading can use simple textbooks, tradebooks, children's reference books, or children's newspapers or magazines. Obviously, a slow-learning child needs much teacher help in picking out the materials that he can read easily and which will help him plan the information which he needs for studying his part of the unit. A slow-learning child probably can present his material to the rest of the class or to his group orally since he may have more difficulty in writing it effectively.

A VAKT or kinesthetic method can be useful with some slow-learning children in the intermediate grades. As was discussed in Chapter 4, the Fernald Tracing Method seems to be more useful since it traces words in syllables instead of tracing isolated sounds.

As in the primary grades, programmed materials in the form of programmed workbooks or teaching machines can be of value in the intermediate grades in reviewing word recognition skills. Programmed materials let slow-learning children experience instant success, have meaningful concrete repetition, and learn materials which have been divided into small orderly units. Depending on the reading level of slow learners in the intermediate grades, the following materials may be of some value: *Sullivan Programmed*

---

[4] T. Hegge, Samuel Kirk, and Winifred Kirk, *Remedial Reading Drills,* Ann Arbor, Michigan: George Wahr, Publisher, 1955; Glenn McCracken and Charles E. Walcutt, *Lippincott Basic Reading Program.* Philadelphia: J. B. Lippincott Company, 1963; Theodore L. Harris, Mildred Creekmore, and Margaret Greenman, *Phonetic Keys to Reading.* Oklahoma City: The Economy Company, 1964.

Reading, Reading, and the *Macmillan Reading Spectrum.*[5] However, slow-learning children need quite a bit of direction in learning how to use programmed materials effectively on their own.

The individualized reading plan can be helpful in motivating intermediate-grade slow-learning children to improve their reading skills and to read more widely. The individualized reading plan is illustrated in Chapter 8. Slow-learning children can use self-selected materials such as tradebooks, easy textbooks, language-experience stories, children's magazines and newspaper and high interest, low vocabulary books. High interest, low vocabulary books have an interest level which is higher than their reading level. A list of high interest, low vocabulary books is found in Appendix VIII. Slow learners need considerable guidance even at the intermediate-grade level in choosing interesting materials that they can read very easily. Individualized reading can be used several days a week for slow-learning children in the intermediate grades.

In the later intermediate grades, the reading of practical materials can be begun. Such reading can help these children to be successful in the practical reading needs that they will encounter later in their lives. Such practical needs are learning to read a job application, the telephone directory, the newspaper, and simple magazines which might relate to a later job.

The language-experience approach also can be useful in the reading program of intermediate-grade slow-learning children. As an example, a sixth-grade girl may want to learn how to bake a cake. Since she may not be able to read and understand the directions for baking the cake, the teacher can read the directions aloud to her and discuss what they mean with her. The student then can dictate the directions in her own words to the teacher who writes them down. The teacher can later type the directions on an index card or on a sheet of notebook paper, and the student then can keep a file of simplified directions which she can read for herself later. Such dictated directions easily can be used in a number of subject matter areas.

Slow learners in the intermediate grades need to see their

---

[5]See: Cynthia Dee Buchanan, *Sullivan Programmed Reading.* St. Louis: Webster Division, McGraw-Hill Book Company, 1963; M. W. Sullivan, *Reading.* Palo Alto, California: Behavioral Research Laboratories, 1965; Lee C. Deighton and Adrian B. Sanford, *The Macmillan Reading Spectrum.* New York: The Macmillan Company, 1964.

reading progress concretely although perhaps not as much as they do in the primary grades. However, they often need motivation in the form of progress charts or in some other concrete way. They also need a patient, understanding teacher who lets them always experience success to help build a good self-concept for them. They can make good steady progress in reading if their program always is on their own level and if they are always able to experience success in it. Obviously, they will never achieve as well as will a more intelligent child, but they can learn to read effectively to achieve some place in society if their teacher helps them.

Characteristics of the Reluctant Reader

Elementary schools today have many reluctant readers in both the later primary grades and in the intermediate grades. In general, elementary schools in the United States have done a fairly good job of teaching word recognition and comprehension skills to most children. However, there are far too many reluctant readers in today's elementary classrooms. We have not done a very good job in motivating some children to want to improve their reading or just simply to want to read at all.

An able reluctant reader is a child who can read adequately but does not want to do so. Sometimes disabled readers are considered to be reluctant readers, but often they would read if they had the skills to do so. Most often a reluctant reader either can read adequately or very well but he just chooses not to read.

There can be a number of reasons which cause a child to be a reluctant reader. He may come from a home where reading is not thought to be of value and his parents provide him with a poor reading model. There also may be no interesting books, magazines or newspapers in the home which would motivate him to read. A child also may be a reluctant reader because his teachers never have shown him that reading is "fun." They could have done this by giving him easy reading materials in some of his areas of interest, by providing him with plenty of free school time in which to read, and by often reading to him in school. Many reluctant readers probably have the impression that reading is really work.

In any case many elementary teachers find the reluctant readers in their classroom to be their greatest challenge since they cannot discover effective ways to motivate them to want to read. It is indeed frustrating to teach students who can read well but who just will not read.

Working with the Reluctant Reader in the Elementary School

Unfortunately there really are no magical answers for how to motivate reluctant readers to read more widely. Obviously, one of the most effective ways is to give them much easy reading material in their own areas of interest. The material always should be very easy for them to read since reading then will seem more like fun. However, the material must not appear babyish to a reluctant reader since this will destroy any interest that he has in reading it. High interest, low vocabulary books sometimes can be used quite effectively with a reluctant reader to motivate him to read. A list of high interest, low vocabulary books is found in Appendix VIII.

Any real interest which a reluctant reader has should be capitalized on in motivating him to read. As an example, a sixth-grade boy who is interested in football perhaps can be given several books on football on his independent or free reading level by either his physical education or classroom teacher. However, the use of a child's interests in selecting reading material for him certainly does not guarantee that he will want to read, but it still is one of the best ways to achieve success in motivating a reluctant reader.

If a child has no real interest, the teacher will have to develop an interest for him before she can give him reading material about the interest. For example, an intermediate-grade boy may be encouraged to develop an interest in the study of rocks after his teacher has brought a display of rocks into the classroom. He then may be encouraged to study rocks from science textbooks or tradebooks on his instructional and independent reading levels. The developing of an interest does not always insure reading success for reluctant readers, but it too can be effective at times.

A classmate can sometimes recommend a book to a reluctant reader. As an example, if there is a class leader whom the reluctant reader admires, the child can be encouraged to tactfully tell the reluctant reader how interesting and "great" a certain book is. The reluctant reader then may want to read the book. Book clubs and very informal book reports also may motivate reluctant readers to read more widely.

The teacher who truly values reading also can motivate the children in her class to value reading. Probably the best way in which the teacher can show her class that she really does value reading is for her to read aloud to them at least once a day throughout the elementary school grades. It is very important for the intermediate-grade teacher to read aloud to her children every day, and it is an unfortunate intermediate-grade classroom that does not hear worthwhile material read aloud by an enthusiastic teacher every day.

If there is a central library with a librarian in the elementary school, the librarian also can be of value in motivating a reluctant reader to read more extensively. The librarian should be told each child's reading level by being given his reading score either from a standardized survey reading test (being told that these scores often overestimate the actual reading level) or from an individual reading inventory. The librarian can find out something about any reluctant reader's interests by talking to him in the school library if the teacher allows the time for doing this. Hopefully, the librarian then can recommend the right books for the reluctant reader.

Probably another important factor in motivating a reluctant reader is the teacher-child relationship. If the teacher has been able to establish very good rapport with a reluctant reader, and he knows that she really respects and likes him, he often may make an effort to read more widely if he knows that she values reading. He later may want to read more widely for his own reasons, but a good teacher-child relationship can be used as a motivating force in the beginning.

It should again be emphasized that there are no foolproof solutions to the motivating of reluctant readers, but it is important that each classroom teacher tries to do this as well as she can. If children do not develop a real liking for reading by the time they leave the intermediate grades, they may well be reluctant readers all of their lives. Think of the great waste of this both in terms of the gaining of information and enjoyment from books.

Characteristics of the Culturally Disadvantaged Child

There have always been a number of culturally disadvantaged

children in our society, but the awareness of their special difficulties has been in the educational focus for the past several years. Culturally disadvantaged children also can be called culturally deprived children or culturally different children. In some ways the less commonly used term culturally different children may be the most accurate since such children have had many experiences in their homes, but not had the kind of experiences which can help them to achieve success in school. Culturally disadvantaged children are found in the inner parts of the large urban centers, in various rural areas in the Midwest and South, in the Appalachian area, and on Indian reservations. Culturally disadvantaged children can be economically poor children but also can include children from various minority groups. Sometimes a disadvantaged child can be both poor and from a minority group.

Culturally disadvantaged children usually use a restricted language style which is a manner of speaking in which they use short sentences, few adjectives and adverbs, few complex verbs, an imprecise vocabulary, and incorrect grammar. They have learned this restricted language style by imitation of their parents and older brothers and sisters in their home. Therefore, they cannot understand the more elaborated language style used by their teachers who generally come from the middle class.

They often come from homes which do not contain many objects to help them to learn vocabulary terms and to build concept. For example, how can a preschool child learn what the term "picture" means if he has never seen a picture on the wall in his house? It is obvious that culturally disadvantaged children have not had many of the kinds of experiences which would help them to understand what they read effectively. Such kinds of experiences could be going on family trips, going to the museum, or going to the zoo. Disadvantaged children often have few books in their homes to look at while they are young or to read when they are older. They often have few materials to work with such as drawing paper, crayons, scissors, paste, or paints.

The parents of disadvantaged children often provide a very poor reading model for their children, and there are few books and magazines in their home. Often the parents do not show much interest in reading and therefore do not provide much motivation for their children in learning to read or in improving their reading skills. Many disadvantaged parents want immediate rewards for their efforts and do not see the value of their children's getting an education, since the rewards then must be delayed for some time. They probably transfer this attitude to their children who therefore see little value in education but see more value in getting a job as soon as they can and earning money.

Often there is little parent-child interaction in the culturally disadvantaged home. When parents speak to their children, they often speak in commands and do not give any reasons for the commands. For example, the parent of a disadvantaged child is more likely to say "Shut up" to his child than he is to say "Would you please be quiet so that I can hear the television program." Disadvantaged families often are large, and the parents have little time to talk individually with their children.

The housing of the disadvantaged often is substandard. Disadvantaged families usually live in crowded conditions due to their family size and to the type of housing which they can afford. Sometimes their homes are noisy and confusing, teaching the children to "tune out" what is going on in the home. Disadvantaged children often carry this trait into the elementary classroom also.

Culturally disadvantaged children often are passive because they have been ordered around so much at home and have been subjected to so much physical punishment. They sometimes have a negative self-concept and think they cannot be successful in school. A culturally disadvantaged child usually enters the primary grades poorly equipped to profit from reading instruction, and he often falls farther and farther behind as he progresses through the elementary grades.

A Reading Program for Primary Grade, Culturally Disadvantaged Children

Generally, a reading program which enables disadvantaged children to actively participate in their own learning seems to be the best for them. They need a reading program which requires active involvement and life-like situations. Disadvantaged children also need a teacher who possesses special characteristics. Their teacher should be able to accept them with their strengths and weaknesses and begin reading instruction for them at the point at which they can experience sure success. They always need to experience success since they usually enter school with a poor self-concept. However, the teacher must never underestimate a disadvantaged child's potential ability. Disadvantaged children often do not score well on standardized group or individual intelligence tests since such tests measure a child's background of experiences and his reading ability as well as his intelligence. Therefore, the teacher may believe that he cannot learn to read effectively and not give him much challenge to do so. Certainly a disadvantaged child generally only achieves as well as his teacher thinks that he is going to achieve.

The language-experience approach can be used very effectively with disadvantaged children to begin reading instruction and as a valuable supplement later on. The language-experience approach is described in detail in Chapter 8, but it uses child-dictated and child-written experience stories and child-dictated experience charts. It is very good to use with disadvantaged children since it uses their own langauage patterns and reflects their own experiences. It shows each child that his oral language is worthwhile and makes him feel important when he sees it written down. The language-experience approach also is valuable because disadvantaged children very often do not have the experiences which the basal readers require for effective comprehension.

Each child's experience stories can be bound into a booklet after his teacher has typed them for him on a primary typewriter and he has illustrated them using crayons, paints, or colored chalk. Sometimes a disadvantaged child can be photographed by his teacher, and then he can dictate or write his experience stories about what he is doing in the photograph. The use of his own photographs can help to build his self-confidence and self-concept which he needs very much.

There is some disagreement about whether the oral language patterns of a disadvantaged child should be changed by the teacher when she is transcribing an experience story for him. Sometimes disadvantaged children use very incorrect grammar and some words which are not acceptable to a teacher of the middle class. Some authorities say that if the teacher rejects any part of a child's oral language, she rejects him. Other authorities say that she can change some words or grammatical usage if she has good rapport with the child and does it in a very tactful way. Probably extremely substandard grammar or offensive words can be changed by the teacher while she transcribes an experience story if she does it tactfully. It is the responsibility of the school to provide ways for disadvantaged children to improve themselves.

There are some special readers for the disadvantaged which can be used to teach the various word recognition and comprehension skills. They follow the same teaching methods as do the regular basal readers which are discussed in Chapter 8. The basal reader method consists of the following steps: presentation of vocabulary and development of a background of experiences, guided silent reading, purposeful oral reading, extending skills and abilities, and enriching experiences.

These special basal readers are supposed to reflect inner-city experiences and use the language patterns of culturally disadvantaged children. Actually, they do not portray inner-city life very realistically nor do they use the language patterns of disadvantaged children. However, they do portray urban living to an extent and use illustrations or photographs of minority group children. These special materials are the *Bank Street Readers* written by the staff of the Bank Street College of Education in New York, the *Chandler Language-Experience Readers* which use urban San Francisco as a setting, and the *City Schools Reading Program* written by the staff of the Detroit Public Schools.[6] These materials should not be used in isolation but with other materials.

Individualized instruction using the individualized reading plan, unit work, and self-directive dramatization may be very useful with disadvantaged children to give practice on the reading skills which have been taught by the use of the language-experience approach or the especially prepared reading materials for the disadvantaged. The individualized reading plan is described in detail in Chapter 8, but it is based upon Willard Olson's philosophy of self-selection, seeking, and self-pacing of reading materials.[7]

In individualized reading a child chooses reading material which he wants to read on his own reading level and reads it

---

[6]See: Bank Street College of Education, *Bank Street Readers,* New York: The Macmillan Company, 1965-1966; Lawrence Carrillo, et al., *Chandler Language Experience Readers.* San Francisco: Chandler Publishing Company, 1964-1966; Detroit Public Schools, *City Schools Reading Program.* Chicago: Follett Publishing Company, 1962-1966.

[7]Willard Olson, *Reading as a Function of Total Growth of the Child.* Chicago: University of Chicago Press, 1940, pp. 233-237.

independently. These materials can be tradebooks, textbooks, language-experience stories, children's reference books, and children's newspapers and magazines. The use of individualized reading with disadvantaged children motivates them to read and creates a love of reading for them because they choose interesting materials for themselves. It also is valuable for them because the one-to-one relationship with the teacher in the individual reading conference makes them feel important and helps them develop a good self-concept.

The unit plan can be used to help individualized reading instruction for disadvantaged children. They can read about a topic or a question which they have chosen to study or which their teacher has asked them to study. They can read about the topic on their own reading level from simple textbooks, tradebooks, or reference materials. They then can tell the rest of the class or group about their findings orally. The use of the unit plan can help disadvantaged children to experience success by letting them work on their own level and by giving them the opportunity to work cooperatively with other children.

The self-directive dramatization can be of use in improving the self-concept and reading ability of disadvantaged children. The self-directive dramatization was developed by Lessie Carlton and Robert Moore of Illinois State University and is described as: "The pupil's own original, imaginative, spontaneous interpretation of a character of his own choosing in a story which he selected and read cooperatively with other pupils in his group which was formed for the time being and for one particular story only."[8]

The self-directive dramatization is quite related to role playing which also can be very beneficial for culturally disadvantaged children. Role playing enables them to learn how to act in some particular situation by actually doing it.

Programmed materials in the form of programmed workbooks or teaching machines can be of value with primary-grade disadvantaged children since they give them immediate reward or reinforcement which is very good for disadvantaged children. The following programmed materials can be used with disadvantaged

---

[8]Lessie Carlton and Robert H. Moore, *Reading, Self-Directive Dramatization and Self-Concept.* Columbus, Ohio: Charles E. Merrill Publishing Company, 1968, p. 10.

children: *Programmed Reading, Lift Off to Reading,* and *Reading in High Gear.*[9]

In summary, the language-experience approach can be used to introduce reading instruction in the primary grades since it effectively uses the experiences and language patterns of disadvantaged children. This approach also can be used as a worthwhile supplement in the later primary grades. The specially prepared basal readers can be used to teach the various word recognition and comprehension skills to culturally disadvantaged children, while individualized reading effectively can reinforce and give practice in the reading skills. The self-directive dramatization, role playing, and programmed materials also have an important place in the reading program for primary-grade, disadvantaged children.

A Reading Program for Intermediate Grade, Culturally Disadvantaged Children

Most of the points made in relation to teacher characteristics and teaching strategies for primary-grade disadvantaged children also are true for disadvantaged children in the intermediate grades. Their reading program should involve as much participation as possible and should be as lifelike as it can be. They also need a teacher who genuinely respects them and can see their potential quite clearly. She must not underestimate their ability to make good improvement. In the intermediate grades culturally disadvantaged children often are reading two or more years below grade level even if they have normal intellectual ability.

The language-experience approach can be used very effectively with non-reading and poorly-reading culturally disadvantaged children at the intermediate-grade level. It is mainly effective because such children can dictate stories to their teacher about the experiences which they actually have had and this motivates them to want to learn to read. Of course, the language-experience approach also uses their own language patterns, which is beneficial to them.

The language-experience approach can use many kinds of experiences as the basis for reading material. As an example, one

---

[9]See: Cynthia Dee Buchanan, *Sullivan Programmed Reading.* St. Louis: Webster Division, McGraw-Hill Book Company, 1963; Myron Woolman, *Lift Off to Reading.* Chicago: Science Research Associates, 1966; Myron Woolman, *Reading In High Gear.* Chicago: Science Research Associates, 1965.

Job Corps Center for high school girls used the language-experience approach to teach reading. At this level, the girls dictated experience stories about what they wanted to do when they got out of the Job Corps such as being a waitress or beautician. The reader thus can see how versatile this approach is, and how it can be used with disadvantaged children in the intermediate grades. At this level, disadvantaged students may or may not want to bind their experience stories into booklets and illustrate them. In any case, the teacher usually should type the experience stories for the more disabled readers as they seem to be more meaningful to them in a typed form. The same point that was made earlier about the harm of changing a disadvantaged child's oral language as the teacher transcribes it also is worth considering for students in the intermediate grades. Whether or not the teacher does try to change the language as she transcribes an experience story probably must depend upon the child and the relationship which the teacher has been able to form with him.

There are no special basal readers to use with disadvantaged children in the intermediate grades at this time. In teaching the various word recognition and comprehension skills, the teacher probably will have to rely on ordinary basal readers at each child's instructional reading level, special supplementary phonics materials, or perhaps high interest, low vocabulary books. If basal readers are used for the teaching of reading skills, the teacher must be sure that they always are on the child's instructional reading level, and she may try to use only those stories which might have the most appeal to disadvantaged children. Special phonics materials such as are described in Chapter 8 sometimes can be used to teach certain phonetic analysis skills to disadvantaged students. However, the teacher must remember that many disadvantaged children have poor auditory discrimination (the ability to hear the likenesses and differences in sounds) and therefore may not do well in any kind of formal phonics programs.

Individualized reading also can be used with intermediate-grade disadvantaged children very effectively. Individualized reading always should be done on the child's independent or free reading level and can use high interest, low vocabulary books, tradebooks, experience stories, textbooks, children's reference books, or children's magazines and newspapers. A list of high interest, low vocabulary books is found in Appendix VIII. Individualized reading can be used two or three days a week in the intermediate grades especially with those disadvantaged students who know how to read fairly well. Individualized reading can provide disadvantaged children with a very good motivation to read more widely, and they often can profit very much from the teacher-pupil relationship in the individual reading conference. Role playing of stories which they have read also can be a useful motivation for the disadvantaged to read more widely. Book clubs and other informal ways of telling their classmates about books which they have read also can motivate disadvantaged children.

The unit plan, especially in the areas of social studies, science, and health, also can be used to individualize reading instruction for disadvantaged children in the intermediate grades. Such children can do research reading on a topic or question which they have chosen for themselves or which the teacher has chosen for them. They can read about the topic or question on their instructional or independent reading level from textbooks, tradebooks, children's reference books, or children's magazines or newspapers. At this level they can report their findings to the rest of the class or the group either in written or oral form.

Programmed materials are supposed to be good to use with culturally disadvantaged children since they provide the immediate reinforcement which these children seem to need. Unfortunately, there are few programmed materials at the intermediate-grade reading level. Such materials mainly can be used only with children in the intermediate grades who read below that level. The programs mentioned in the preceding section would be good for such children.

The disadvantaged child in the intermediate grades almost must experience success in reading. Therefore, he must always read on his instructional or independent reading levels. The language-experience approach may be useful with intermediate-grade disadvantaged children who read below grade level. The various word recognition and comprehension skills can mainly be presented by using regular basal reader materials at the child's instructional reading level. Individualized instruction in the form of individualized reading, role playing, unit work, and programmed materials can serve to reinforce the reading skills learned in another way.

SUMMARY

This chapter discussed slow-learning children, able reluctant readers, and culturally disadvantaged children at the elementary-school level. Slow-learning children do not show much curiosity and often appear to be passive and withdrawn in school especially if the school tasks are too difficult for them. They usually should not recieve formal reading instruction before the chronological age of eight. The program for slow-learning children in the primary grades can consist of the development of visual perception, the use of the language-experience approach, the basal reader or a formal phonics approach, a kinesthetic method, programmed materials, and individualized reading. Each of these methods has some special strength which can help slow-learning children to reach their ultimate potential in reading.

The program for slow-learning children in the intermediate grades can consist of the basal reader approach, supplementary phonics materials, the unit plan, a kinesthetic method, programmed reading, individualized reading, and possibly the language-experience approach. Slow-learning children can learn to read adequately if the program is geared to their special needs and abilities.

Reluctant readers are those children who can read adequately or very well but do not want to do so. Elementary classrooms contain far too many reluctant readers. There are no foolproof solutions on how to motivate a reluctant reader to learn to read more widely. However, the following ways may be of some value: using a child's interests in helping him find books to read, reading aloud to the class every day, developing interests for him, and the teacher-child relationship.

Culturally disadvantaged children often use a restricted language style, have had few experiences which help them to understand the materials found in the basal readers, have had little parent-child interaction, and are not ready for most school experiences. The reading program for culturally disadvantaged children in the primary grades can consist of the language-experience approach, special basal readers for the disadvantaged, individualized reading, the self-directive dramatization, and programmed reading materials.

The reading program for intermediate-grade culturally disadvantaged children can use the basal reader approach, much individualized reading perhaps using some high-interest, low-vocabulary books, role-playing, unit work, and programmed reading materials. The reading program always should let disadvantaged children be actively involved, and the teacher should never fail to believe that disadvantaged children are able to make good progress in reading.

REFERENCES

Cheyney, Arnold B. *Teaching Culturally Disadvantaged in the Elementary School.* Columbus, Ohio: Charles E. Merrill Publishing Company, 1967.

Dechant, Emerald V. *Diagnosis and Remediation of Reading Disability.* West Nyack, New York: Parker Publishing Company, Incorporated, 1968. Chapter 6.

Horn, Thomas D. (Editor) *Reading for the Disadvantaged.* New York: Harcourt, Brace and World, Incorporated, 1970.

Miller, Wilma H. *The First R: Elementary Reading Today.* New York: Holt, Rinehart and Winston, Incorporated, 1972. Chapter 17.

Zintz, Miles V. *Corrective Reading.* Dubuque, Iowa: William C. Brown Company, Publishers, 1966. Chapter 5.

8

Modern Elementary Reading Approaches

This chapter includes a brief survey of all the modern approaches to elementary reading instruction which are used in the United States at the present time. The chapter is not designed to take the place of a book on elementary reading instruction, but rather to give the reader a brief overview of some of the methods which can be used with various children in a corrective reading program.

The chapter describes the basal reader approach, the language-experience approach, the individualized reading plan, some formal phonics programs, the initial teaching alphabet, the diacritical marking system, the linguistic approaches, words in color, programmed and computer-based reading instruction, and an approach which emphasizes neurological dominance. It illustrates some of the uses of these approaches in a reading improvement program. The chapter also includes a very brief discussion of some of the grouping methods which can be used in elementary reading instruction.

The Basal Reader Approach

Most readers probably are familiar with the basal reader approach from their childhood experiences and teaching experiences. Basal readers are the most widely-used reading materials in the United States at the present time. Nearly every primary-grade classroom and most intermediate-grade classrooms use the basal reader approach as one way to teach reading.

The basal reader approach uses a series of textbooks beginning at the reading readiness level and continuing through the sixth or eighth grade reading levels to teach the various word recognition and comprehension skills. The reading readiness level usually contains a reading readiness workbook which is designed to teach the readiness skills of visual and auditory discrimination, picture interpretation, left-to-right progression, and the development of a background of experiences. In first grade reading instruction is introduced by using three or four soft-covered books called preprimers, the accompanying teacher's manuals, picture and word cards, and a large book, a representation of the first preprimer. In first grade word recognition usually is begun with the presentation of picture clues and word form clues such as configuration:

About seventy-five to one hundred words are learned by sight before the children are introduced to other word recognition techniques. After a group of children has completed the three or four preprimers, they are introduced to their first hard-covered book called a primer. They also often read a first reader in first grade. In the primer and first reader, the rudimentary elements of phonetic analysis and structural analysis are presented.

In second and third grade, there are two basal readers for each grade. Reading for meaning receives great emphasis at this level as it did from the earliest stages in first grade. Phonetic analysis skills receive greatly increased stress in second grade and refinement in third grade, while the structural analysis skills presented in first grade are extended and refined in second and third grade.

In the fourth through the sixth grades, or possibly through the eighth grade, there is one basal reader for each year. Comprehension continues to receive stress and phonetic and structural analysis skills, the use of context clues, and dictionary usage receive continued refinement and application. The emphasis shifts from "learning to read" to "reading to learn."

In all basal reader series the basal reader lessons follow about the same teaching method. They usually follow this format: development of a background of experiences, presentation of vocabulary, guided silent reading, purposeful oral reading, extending skills and abilities, and enriching experiences. The basal reader approach traditionally has featured the use of three reading achievement groups: the fast-moving group, the average group, and the slow-moving group. In first grade the division usually is made on the basis of teacher evaluation and a reading readiness or group intelligence test. In the later primary and intermediate grades the classification often is made on the basis of teacher evaluation and standardized survey reading or achievement tests. Although the teacher's manuals of all basal reader series stress that reading achievement grouping should remain flexible, in practice the reading achievement groups are quite fixed because the reading skills are presented in a developmental, sequential manner.

The basal reader approach does have uses in a corrective reading program. All of the word recognition and comprehension skills are presented in a developmental and logical way in the various teacher's manuals. For the nonreader, the teacher can be sure that all of the reading skills are presented if she follows the basal reader approach carefully. For disabled readers with specific weaknesses, only those word recognition and comprehension skills in which a child has been found to be weak in should be presented to him. However, the basal reader approach with its readers and teacher's manuals can well be used for such a purpose. The regular workbooks and special phonics workbooks found in basal reader series provide a useful review of the skills taught during the fourth part of the basal reader lesson. They can save time for the teacher in locating independent work activities for a disabled reader or a group of readers. Only those workbook pages should be used which will reinforce the reading skills that a disabled reader or a group of them found themselves to be weak in. In general, the content and format of basal reading is quite appealing to many of the children who are to use them, with the exception being older severely disabled readers. For them, the content of the basal readers on their instructional levels probably would appear too "babyish." The interests of boys now are being considered in developing new basal readers, while the interest of culturally disadvantaged children are somewhat reflected in the basal readers which were designed for them and were described in Chapter 7.

However, a teacher can follow the teacher's manuals much too closely, and thus her creativity can be limited and she may not individualize reading instruction as much as she might. Teacher's manuals should only be used as a source of suggestions by all but the most inexperienced teachers. Even when the basal reader approach is used as the major reading approach in a corrective reading program, the disabled reader also should do much additional reading from tradebooks, language-experience stories, subject matter textbooks, children's reference books, and children's newspapers and magazines on his instructional or independent reading levels. Of course, the grade level designation on a basal reader should not be any indication that all children at that grade level can read it effectively. All disabled readers should receive instruction on their instructional reading level as determined from an Individual Reading Inventory which was described in Chapter 3. This will often be a basal reader one or more years below the grade in which the disabled reader is currently in. The extreme vocabulary control especially in the beginning basal readers makes their language patterns not much like the actual oral language of children in the elementary school. However, currently there is less vocabulary control in basal readers than there was in the past since more linguistic knowledges are being applied to this approach.

The basal reader approach should be only one way in which a teacher works with a disabled reader or group of disabled readers in a corrective reading program. It should be used in combination with several other approaches such as the language-experience approach and the individualized reading plan, or with a supplementary phonics approach and individualized reading depending upon each child's or group of children's special reading needs.

The Language-Experience Approach

The language-experience approach is one of the most versatile and useful reading approaches in a corrective reading program. This approach has a number of unique advantages which make it valuable for use in beginning reading and in combination with several other approaches later on. It is especially valuable with disabled readers and culturally disadvantaged children.

The language-experience approach consists both of individually dictated and written experience stories and group-dictated experience charts. One of its major proponents is R. Van Allen of the University of Arizona who has crystallized it in the following way:

> What I can think about, I can say.
> What I can say, I can write.
> I can read what I have written.
> I can read what others have written for me to read.[1]

The language-experience approach can be begun at the reading readiness level when the teacher asks the child to dictate a story to her about one of his own experiences. The teacher transcribes the story on an index card or on a large sheet of chart paper. If she has transcribed it on an index card, she often will later type it on a primary typewriter and give it back to the child to illustrate and to "read" with her. If she transcribed it on a sheet of chart paper, she and the child together "read" it while she emphasizes left-to-right progression and the learning of a few words by sight.

A group of children or an entire class can dictate experience charts which the teacher transcribes on the chalkboard or a piece of chart paper. If she has transcribed it on the chalkboard, she later will rewrite it on a piece of chart paper using a magic marker or a felt-tipped pen. At the later first-grade reading level, individual children can begin to write their own experience stories, and they are encouraged to spell the words they need in the ways in which they think they should be spelled. In the case of either child-dictated or child-written experience stories, the child can illustrate his own experience stories and bind them into a booklet. He then can make a cover for the booklet and take it home to his parents to read to them.

As a child progresses through the later primary-grade reading levels, the language-experience approach mainly is used as a supplement as he writes his own experience stories and reads them and those of his classmates. The approach often is used in combination with another approach such as the basal reader approach, a formal phonics method, or words in color. The children using the language-experience approach also read basal

---

[1] Dorris Lee and R. Van Allen, *Learning to Read Through Experience.* New York: Appleton-Century-Crofts, 1963, p. 2.

readers and supplementary books, tradebooks, textbooks, children's reference books, and children's newspapers and magazines on a predominantly individualized basis.

The language experience approach is an excellent way to develop reading readiness and to begin a program of reading instruction for disabled readers since it enables them to understand that "reading really is just talk written down." Obviously, the approach uses the child's own experiences as the basis of his reading materials so he always can understand what he reads. This is especially important for disadvantaged children as was discussed in Chapter 7. The language-experience approach also uses each child's own unique language patterns. Children can read their own language patterns much more effectively than they can read anyone else's language patterns. This is especially true in the case of disabled readers and disadvantaged children. A child's creativity also is enhanced because of the ways in which the various art media can be used in illustrating the experience stories and in making covers for the experience booklet. The approach very effectively stresses the interrelationships between the language arts of listening speaking, reading, and writing. The approach also creates a real interest in learning to read and is therefore very valuable for use with older nonreaders even at the adult level.

The language-experience approach has a number of limitations when used as the only approach in a corrective reading program. However, all of these limitations do not exist when the approach is used in combination with another more structured approach since the basal reading approach or another approach emphasizes the decoding aspects of reading. Its most important limitation is its lack of sequential skill development of the word recognition skills of phonetic analysis and structural analysis. Since it does not have vocabulary control, a child may never learn the basic sight words unless his teacher makes a special effort to present them individually to him or in a small group of children. The approach seems to be quite unstructured for the inexperienced teacher although there are now some materials available which can help a teacher learn how to use the approach effectively.[2] A child must have many experiences so that they have much to talk about, and the teacher must have many reading

[2]R. Van Allen and Claryce Allen, *Language Experience in Reading.* Chicago: Encyclopaedia Britannica Press, 1966.

materials and materials to use in making the language-experience booklets available in her classroom.

The Individualized Reading Plan

Individualized reading has received much emphasis during the past ten years and is one of the more widely-known elementary reading approaches in the United States at the present time. However, individualized instruction really dates from the 1920's when it was used in such cities as Madison, Wisconsin, Pueblo, Colorado, and Winnetka, Illinois. Individualized reading as it is known today is based on the philosophy of Willard Olson, a child development specialist, who believed that reading ability always is a part of a child's total development. He stated that each child seeks to read, should select his own reading materials, and should pace his own reading.[3] It is difficult to describe pure individualized reading since some of the teachers who say they use individualized reading really use some modified or combination plan which features the use of some individualized reading. Pure individualized reading at the first-grade reading level sometimes uses the language-experience approach to introduce reading instruction. When a child has learned a few words by sight from language-experience stories and charts, he then reads his first simple tradebook at his desk or with the teacher in the individual reading conference. When he has read the first tradebook, he then chooses another tradebook to read.

When a pure individualized reading plan is used at the later primary grade reading level, a child chooses the books which he wants to read and can read easily. Usually these books are on his independent or free reading level. He keeps a record of the books he reads by listing the titles and authors of the books and by writing several sentences about the content of the books. He keeps these records on simple duplicated sheets, index cards, or in a looseleaf notebook. He can meet with his teacher two or three times a week for ten to fifteen minutes in an individual reading conference when he reads a portion of the book aloud to his teacher, and she asks him factual and higher-type comprehension questions about it. During the conference the teacher also diag-

[3]Willard Olson, *Reading as a Function of the Total Growth of the Child.* Chicago: University of Chicago Press, 1940.

noses and possibly corrects word recognition and comprehension difficulties. She also keeps a record of the child's reading by listing the titles and authors of the books he has read and by noting his specific word recognition and comprehension difficulties on a page she has for him in a looseleaf notebook. The teacher can call short-term needs groups together when she has decided that certain children who read on the same level have a common skill weakness such as poor knowledge of the short vowel sounds. In the individualized reading plan a child can read tradebooks, language-experience stories, simple reference books, subject matter textbooks, and children's magazines and newspapers.

The individualized reading plan is conducted quite similarly at the intermediate-grade reading level. At this level the child also self-selects and self-paces his reading. Individualized reading may take the place of the basal reader approach at this level, but a child needs to do considerable additional reading of subject matter materials. At the intermediate-grade reading level a child probably meets with his teacher twice a week for a ten to fifteen minute individual reading conference. Probably less oral reading is done during the conference at the intermediate-grade reading level, and the child mainly tells the teacher about the contents of the book he has read and his reaction to it. The teacher probably asks him various higher-type comprehension questions about it. She also diagnoses and sometimes corrects the word recognition and comprehension difficulties which she notices that the child has. The child keeps a record of what he has read on duplicated forms, index cards, or in a notebook including the titles and authors of the books, a short summary of them, and his critical reactions to them. The teacher also keeps records of a child's reading often in a looseleaf notebook with a page for each child. She lists the titles and authors of the books and the child's specific word recognition and comprehension weakness. The reading materials for individualized reading at the intermediate-grade reading level can be found in basal reader stories from many grade levels, subject matter textbooks, tradebooks in many areas of interests and on many different reading levels, magazines and newspapers, and children's reference books. The teacher may form short-term groups to teach certain word recognition or comprehension skills to several children who showed a weakness in them.

Individualized reading has a number of unique advantages

when it is used in its pure form that also can be advantages when individualized reading is used in combination with several other approaches such as the basal reader approach, the language-experience approach, or a formal phonics program. Therefore, individualized reading can very well be used in a corrective reading program. Its main advantage probably is that it creates an interest in reading in a child who is using it since he can self-select and self-pace his own reading. A child who uses individualized reading is very likely to read more widely and to develop many new reading interests. Many disabled readers and disadvantaged children receive great motivation by the undivided teacher attention they get in the one-to-one relationship found in the individual reading conference. Individualized reading may help children to develop their self-reliance and independence since they have to work without direct teacher supervision much of the time each day during the reading period. Individualized reading also may help children to develop their decision-making and problem-solving ability since they have so many alternatives to choose from during the time they work independently.

However, pure individualized reading has a number of limitations, most of which can be eliminated when this plan is used in a corrective reading program in combination with one or several other reading approaches. The major limitation is its lack of sequential skill development especially of the word recognition skills of phonetic analysis and structural analysis. Many elementary teachers seem to need some direction in knowing how to teach the various word recognition and comprehension skills since they do not understand the complex reading process as well as they might. Especially at the first-grade reading level is much teacher time and effort required to teach the word recognition skills on a predominantly individual basis. Individualized reading really requires that a school have a well-equipped central library with reading materials on many different topics and reading levels.

Formal Phonics Programs

American schools have had formal phonics methods of teaching reading for many years. Phonics has been in the educational focus on and off since 1783 when Noah Webster wrote his famous speller. Phonics has received considerable emphasis since 1955 when Rudolph Flesch wrote his very controversial book entitled *Why Johnny Can't Read and What You Can Do About It.*[4] In general, formal phonics programs teach more phonetic rules earlier than do other reading methods and insist phonetic analysis is the most important, if not the only, word recognition technique.

At the present time there are quite a number of formal phonics programs which can be purchased by educators. Each child that uses one of them should have good auditory discrimination (the ability to hear the likenesses and differences in sounds). Many disadvantaged children do not have good auditory discrimination. Some of these formal phonics programs can be used as a major method of teaching elementary reading, while others are supplementary and should be used with other reading approaches such as the basal reader approach, the language-experience approach, or the individualized reading plan. Some of them emphasize comprehension quite a good deal, while others emphasize only word recognition or decoding. Some of the formal phonics programs use synthetic phonetic analysis, the blending of individual sounds into words such as "buh-a-tuh" into the word "bat." Others emphasize analytic phonetic analysis, in which a whole word is first analyzed into syllables and then each syllable is sounded and blended into the word such as "lăd/der." Most reading specialists believe that analytic phonetic analysis is the most meaningful for most children in the elementary school.

Some of the more commonly used formal phonics programs are the following:

(1) *Phonetic Keys to Reading* by Theodore L. Harris, Mildred Creekmore, and Margaret Greenman. Published at Oklahoma City: The Economy Company, 1964.

This is mainly a basic reading program which uses analytic phonetic analysis and stresses comprehension. The program begins at the first-grade level and continues through the intermediate-grade level. The vowels are presented first and the consonants are presented later.

(2) *Open Court Method* by Arthur Trace, et. al. Published by LaSalle, Illinois: The Open Court Company, 1963.

This is a basic reading program which uses writing as an aid to reading. It stresses synthetic phonetic analysis.

(3) *Lippincott Basic Reading Program* by Glenn McCracken and

[4] Rudolph Flesch, *Why Johnny Can't Read.* New York: Harper and Row, Publishers, 1955.

Charles E. Walcutt. Published at Philadelphia: J. B. Lippincott Company, 1963.

This is a basic reading program which uses writing as an aid to reading. It uses synthetic phonetic analysis. At the primary-grade level it mainly uses fables, folktales, and fairy tales as the reading material.

(4) *Reading with Phonics* by Julie Hay and Charles E. Wingo. Published at Philadelphia: J. B. Lippincott Company, 1967.

This is a supplementary phonics program using synthetic phonetic analysis.

(5) *Phonovisual Method* by Luculle D. Schoolfield and Josephine B. Timberlake. Published at Washington, D.C.: Phonovisual Products, 1944.

This is a supplementary phonics program which uses synthetic phonetic analysis.

(6) *Breaking the Sound Barrier* by Sister Mary Caroline. Published at New York: The Macmillan Company, 1960.

This program is supplementary and uses synthetic phonetic analysis.

Formal phonics programs can have some use in a corrective reading program. They can be beneficial to some disabled readers who have good auditory discrimination. A supplementary phonics program, perhaps especially *The Phonovisual Method,* can be a valuable supplement to disabled readers who are learning to read by an approach which does not emphasize the word recognition skills such as the language-experience approach or individualized reading plan. However, all words which a child learns to sound out should be in his oral language vocabulary so that he can always understand what he is reading. A child should not have much training in phonetic analysis until he has reached the mental age of about seven and a half, which a slow-learning child will not do until the chronological age of nine or more. All reading specialists believe that phonetic analysis is one of the most important word recognition techniques, and that a child cannot become an effective reader without mastering them. In the corrective reading program, the teacher can choose a basic or supplementary phonics program at the child's instructional reading level and use only those portions of it which specifically correct his diagnosed weaknesses.

The teacher should realize that a formal phonics program can encourage an emphasis on the sounding out of words to the exclusion of reading for meaning. The use of a formal phonics program is one cause of the word-by-word reading that sometimes is seen in the later primary and intermediate grades.

The Initial Teaching Alphabet

The initial teaching alphabet, sometimes call i/t/a, is a fairly new way to teach beginning reading to first-grade children or to disabled readers who have failed to learn to read by some other method. It is not a method of teaching reading but an artificial alphabet to use in the teaching of reading. The alphabet was developed by Sir James Pitman in England to attempt to correct the somewhat irregular sound-symbol correspondence found in the traditional alphabet.

It consists of forty-four symbols to represent the forty-four sounds in the English language. Figure 8-1 is a copy of this alphabet. You may notice that in this alphabet one sound is represented by one symbol so that the i/t/a alphabet is said to have a regulary phoneme (sound) - grapheme (symbol) relationship, thus making beginning reading instruction easier.

When the i/t/a alphabet is used for reading instruction, several methods of teaching reading can be used. In the beginning stages of reading instruction in England, word form clues commonly are used as the major word recognition technique, while in the United States phonetic analysis is much more commonly used. In the United States the i/t/a materials are called the i/t/a *Early-to-read Series.*[5] In a first grade which is using i/t/a all the labels in the room are written in the i/t/a alphabet with the exception of each child's own name which is written in the traditional alphabet. All the reading materials which the child reads at this stage including tradebooks are written in the i/t/a alphabet. The transition to the traditional alphabet usually is made during the last part of first grade or the first part of second grade.

The i/t/a alphabet may be of value in the corrective reading program for disabled readers who have failed to learn to read by another method. Its novelty may motivate him to want to learn to read. Probably it is best to teach about one hundred words by sight in the i/t/a alphabet before a disabled reader receives much instruction in phonetic analysis. It will not be very costly for the

---

[5] Albert J. Mazurkiewicz and Harold J. Tanyzer, *Early-to-read: i/t/a program.* (New York: Initial Teaching Alphabet Publication, Inc., 1963).

æ	b	c	d	ϵϵ	
face	bed	cat	dog	key	
f	g	h	ie	j	k
feet	leg	hat	fly	jug	key
l	m	n	œ	p	ɹ
letter	man	nest	over	pen	girl
r	s	t	ue	v	w
red	spoon	tree	use	voice	window
y	z	ƨ	wh	ch	
yes	zebra	daisy	when	chair	
th	th	sh	ʒ	ng	
three	the	shop	television	ring	
ɑ	au	a	e	i	o
father	ball	cap	egg	milk	box
u	ω	ω	ou	oi	
up	book	spoon	out	oil	

—Used by permission of
Initial Teaching Alphabet Publications,
New York, N. Y.

FIGURE 8-1

teacher to obtain enough reading materials, including supplementary readers and tradebooks, written in the i/t/a alphabet to use with one child or a small group of children in a corrective reading program. Therefore, the expenditure involved does not become the disadvantage which it is when i/t/a materials are adopted for use in all the first grades in a school system.

The teacher will have to study the initial teaching alphabet before she can teach it effectively, and this may be somewhat time consuming. It may well be worth it if this novel method can motivate disabled readers to learn to read. However, the transition from the i/t/a alphabet to the traditional alphabet may be difficult for some children since they must unlearn a number of concepts.

The Diacritical Marking System

Another attempt to change the irregular sound-symbol relationship found in the English language recently was developed by Edward Fry of Rutgers University. This medium for beginning reading instruction is called the diacritical marking system. It is interesting to note that the first modification of a traditional alphabet was developed by John Hart in England in 1570, and there have been a number of modified alphabets since that time.

Fry takes words and places various diacritical markings above the sounds in them to make the sound-symbol relationship consistent. His diacritical markings are somewhat like those found in the pronunciation guides of dictionaries. When a child has learned to read, the diacritical markings will no longer be used.

Although the diacritical marking system could be of use with a disabled reader who has failed to learn to read by another method, the i/t/a alphabet probably is more useful with a disabled reader. There are more materials presently in the i/t/a alphabet to use than there are in the diacritical marking system.

The Linguistic Reading Approaches

The linguistic methods have been in focus as one of the ways in which beginning reading instruction can be presented for about ten years. There really is no one linguistic method since linguists differ among themselves as to what reading is and how it should be presented. Linguistics is the study of language, and linguists are the scholars who study language. Linguistics is a very complex science; therefore it is difficult to describe linguistic reading approaches so that they can easily be understood. Therefore, perhaps it is easiest to divide the linguistic approaches into two separate areas.

One linguistic approach is called the approach of the phonologists since it emphasizes using a regular phoneme (sound)-grapheme (symbol) relationship in the teaching of reading. Phonologists are represented by the late Charles Fries who has written the *Merrill Linguistic Readers* with his wife and two reading specialists: Henry Lee Smith and Clara Stratemeyer, who have written *The Linguistic Science Readers,* and Leonard Bloomfield and Clarence Barnhart, who have written *Let's Read.*[6]

---

[6]Charles Fries, Agnes Fries, Rosemary G. Wilson, and Mildred K. Rudolph, *Merrill Linguistic Readers.* Columbus, Ohio: Charles E. Merrill Books, Incorporated, 1966; Henry Lee Smith, Junior and Clara G. Stratemeyer, *The Linguistic Science Readers.* New York: Harper and Row, Publishers, 1964; Leonard Bloomfield and Clarence L. Barnhart, *Let's Read.* Bronxville, New York: Clarence L. Barnhart, Incorporated, 1963-1966.

Phonologists emphasize the teaching of words in special patterns, and the use of contrasting spelling patterns to teach new words as the following example illustrates:

man	mane
can	cane
pan	pane
Dan	Dane
fan	fane

The reader can notice that in each case the contrasting spelling pattern was made by adding a silent final "e." Normally it does not matter to phonologists if nonsense syllables are used instead of words in making the contrasting spelling patterns. The sound-symbol relationship also is kept constant in the beginning stages of reading instructions in that spelling patterns containing only the short vowel sounds are used in the beginning books instead of all the other sounds which the vowels can have. However, the sounds never are separated or isolated in the words as is done in a formal phonics program since linguists believe that the sounds then are distorted. Phonologists do not use picture clues as a word recognition technique.

The reading material of the phonologists can be quite useful with disabled readers who are virtually nonreaders and who have good auditory discrimination (the ability to hear the likenesses and differences in sounds). The use of the regular sound-symbol relationship has proven quite useful with such disabled readers. The two best sets of materials probably are *The Linguistic Science Readers* and the *Miami Linguistic Readers.*[7]

The other linguistic view can be called the view of the structuralists, although there is no reading material at the present time which represents their view. However, there probably will be such reading material in the near future. Structuralists emphasize the use of sentence structure, sentence patterns, word function, and word order in the teaching of reading.

Structuralists probably are best represented by Carl Lefevre of Temple University.[8] He believes that reading should be taught

---

[7]Henry Lee Smith, Junior and Clara G. Stratemeyer, *The Linguistic Science Readers.* New York: Harper and Row, Publishers, 1964; *Miami Linguistic Readers.* Boston: D. C. Heath Company, 1964.

[8]Carl A. Lefevre, *Linguistics and the Teaching of Reading.* New York: McGraw-Hill Book Company, 1964.

by using sentence patterns. There are about four unique sentence patterns, and structuralists believe that all reading material at the beginning stage should use the same kind of sentence pattern. A structuralist's view of reading is related to the old "sentence" or "story" method of teaching reading. Since there are no materials at the presnt time representing the structuralist's way of teaching reading, it is obvious that such material does not have a place in the corrective reading program. In any case, it is doubtful that such materials will have much real value in a corrective reading program even when they become available.

Words in Color

Words in Color is a supplementary approach which can be used to teach phonetic analysis or part of the decoding aspect of reading.[9] It is a fairly new approach and was developed by Caleb Gattegno, the originator of the cuisinaire rods used in modern mathematics. Words in Color can be used at the beginning stages of reading instruction in first grade or with older nonreaders. It features a series of large charts which are placed in the elementary classroom. These charts are black with part of the words printed in white and the various phonetic elements within the words printed in different colors. All of the phonetic elements which are pronounced the same are printed in the same color no matter how they are spelled. For example, the long "i" sound in the word "ice" would be printed in the same color as the "i" sound heard in the words "aisle," "pie," "cry," and "sigh."

A child uses color clues found on the chart to learn such phonetic association, but the words in the books which accompany the charts are printed in black on white paper to insure that a child does not rely on color clues for so long that he cannot recognize words without them. It is obvious that Words in Color cannot be used by children who are color blind. Boys are more likely to be color blind than are girls, and boys especially should be given a test of color blindness before the program is begun with them. Words in Color has a place in the corrective reading program with disabled readers who are very weak in phonetic analysis skills and who are not color blind. Usually it should be combined with another approach such as the language-experience approach or

[9] Caleb Gattegno, *Words in Color: Backgrounds and Principles.* Chicago: Learning Materials, Incorporated, of the Encyclopaedia Britannica Press, 1962.

individualized reading. In such a case Words in Color can be used to teach the decoding aspects of reading, while the language-experience approach or individualized reading can be used to teach reading for understanding.

Programmed and Computer-Based Reading Instruction

Programmed instruction has received emphasis in American schools for about the past ten years and has been applied to reading instruction for about eight years. Programmed instruction is based on the theory of B. F. Skinner of Harvard University who stated that if a person is given a stimulus, he will respond to it in some predetermined way.[10] Programmed instruction takes part of the curriculum and divides it into small logically-ordered units that the subject is supposed to respond to. If his answer was correct, he gets some type of signal showing that it was correct, and he then proceeds to the next frame or section of the book. Programmed instruction in reading can use either workbooks, or teaching machines and is best suited to the reviewing of word recognition skills such as phonetic analysis and structural analysis. It is not very well suited to comprehension skills since they are more difficult to program.

Programmed reading materials currently are mainly designed for use at the early stages of reading instruction and they are somewhat linguistically oriented since they use a number of spelling patterns. However, they can be used at later stages of reading instruction especially in the teaching or reviewing of vocabulary. Some early reading programs are *Programmed Reading, The Progressive Choice Reading Program, Reading in High Gear,* and *Lift Off to Reading.*[11] A program for the teaching of vocabulary is *Programmed Vocabulary.*[12]

Programmed reading instruction can be of use in a corrective

---

[10]B.F. Skinner, "Reinforcement Today," *The American Psychologist,* Vol. 13 (March 1958), 94-99.

[11]See: Cynthia D. Buchanan, *Sullivan Programmed Reading* (St. Louis: Webster Division, McGraw-Hill Book Company, 1963); Myron Woolman, *The Progressive Choice Reading Program* (Washington, D. C.: Institute of Educational Research, Inc., 1962); Myron Woolman, *Reading in High Gear* (Chicago: Science Research Associates, 1965); and Myron Woolman, *Lift Off to Reading* (Chicago: Science Research Associates, 1966).

[12]James Brown, *Programmed Vocabulary* (New York: Appleton-Century-Crofts, 1964).

reading program to review some aspects of the word recognitions skills. Such material should not normally be used to teach such skills but rather to review them. If children are given some guidance in how to use programmed material, they can work independently while the teacher is working with other children in the classroom. The immediate reinforcement which they get from using programmed material can be very good with either disadvantaged or slow-learning children.

An Approach Emphasizing Neurological Dominance

The teacher of a corrective reading program often may hear of what is commonly known as "the Delacato approach to the teaching of reading." This theory was developed by Carl Delacato and others at the Institute for the Development of Human Potential in Philadelphia.[13] This theory is based on an understanding of how the brain functions and is difficult to explain simply. However, Delacato believes that a failure to achieve neurological integration below the cortical level of the brain can cause neither side of the brain to develop dominance. Delacato states that one side (hemisphere) of the brain should be dominant for a child to do well in any of the language processes such as speaking and reading. Therefore, Delacato and his associates state that one major cause of reading disability is incompletely developed dominance of one side of the brain.

Delacato and his associates have outlined two plans, one of which is to prevent incompletely developed neurological dominance and the other of which is to correct it. They recommend a program for very young children beginning when they are about six months old. They recommend that the very young child have many opportunities to creep and crawl, not spend a great deal of time in his playpen, and have few restrictions in his clothing. For older disabled readers they recommend cross-pattern creeping and crawling, cross-pattern walking, covering the recessive eye with eye glasses with a piece of red paper on them, positioning the child on his dominant side while he is sleeping, and eliminating music from his environment.

The research studies on the use of this program with disabled

[13] Carl H. Delacato, *The Diagnosis and Treatment of Speech and Reading Problems.* Springfield, Illinois: Charles C. Thomas, 1963.

readers all have been greatly criticized by two research experts, Gene Glass of the University of Colorado and Melvyn P. Robbins of the Ontario Institute for Studies in Education.[14] Therefore, the use of this program cannot be recommended with disabled readers until it has received much additional good research.

Several Methods of Grouping for Reading Instruction

There are several methods of grouping children for elementary reading instruction, some of which probably can be used in some phases of a corrective reading program. Some of these are used in a few elementary reading approaches, while others are used in other reading approaches. The most commonly used form of grouping for elementary reading instruction is called reading achievement grouping in which children are grouped for reading instruction within a classroom on the basis of their reading performance as measured by teacher judgment and standardized reading or achievement tests. The typical elementary classroom uses three reading achievement groups—the fast-moving group, the average group, and the slow-moving group, although a few elementary classrooms have four reading achievement groups. In the average group the children are the most nearly alike within the group. Reading achievement groups should be *flexible* so that children can easily move from group to group, but in practice they are often fixed since the reading skills are so developmental. Reading achievement groups are found in the basal reader approach, formal phonics programs, the initial teaching alphabet, the linguistic reading approaches, and words in color.

Needs or skills groups are short-term flexible groups which the teacher calls when she decides that several children are weak in one or in several word recognition or comprehension skills. As an example, a needs group might be called to learn or to review the consonant blends. When the children have learned the reading skills for which the group was formed, it is no longer used. Needs or skills groups are predominantly used in the language-experience approach and the individualized reading plan.

Interest and research groups are quite similar in many ways.

---

[14]Gene B. Glass and Melvyn P. Robbins, "A Critique of Experiments on the Role of Neurological Organization in Reading Performance," *Reading Research Quarterly*, Volume 3, Fall, 1967, pp. 5-52.

In the interest groups several children decide they want to learn more about a certain topic, while in the research group the teacher assigns the topic. Either group can be composed of good, average, or slow readers. The group then researches the topic at each child's reading level from tradebooks, children's magazines or newspapers, children's reference books, or subject matter textbooks. Either group can report its findings to the rest of the class either in an oral or in a written form. The group no longer functions when it has looked up the interest or the research topic to its satisfaction. Either group can be used in the basal reader approach, the language-experience approach, individualized reading, a formal phonics method, the initial teaching alphabet, or a linguistic approach.

The Joplin Plan is a method of interclass grouping in which children in the intermediate grades are grouped in reading levels according to their reading ability. The Joplin Plan can function in just fourth grades, in just fifth grades, in just sixth grades, or in the fourth, fifth, and sixth grades in an elementary school. The children are divided into reading levels on the basis of standardized reading test scores and teacher judgment. They all have their reading instruction at the same time from the teacher who teaches their reading level. Any elementary reading method or combination of methods can be employed within each level.

The tutorial or "buddy system" consists of a child-teacher and a child-pupil. The child-teacher can teach or review any reading skill which the child-pupil needs some help with. Normally, the child-teacher should review instead of teach reading skills. A tutorial group can be used in any reading method.

SUMMARY

This chapter included a brief survey of all of the approaches to elementary reading instruction which currently are in use in American schools. It gave a brief overview of each of these approaches and indicated how they can be used in a corrective reading program. The chapter also gave a very brief description of some of the methods of grouping for elementary reading instruction.

The basal reader approach is the most widely-used elementary reading approach currently in use in American schools. This approach features a series of reading textbooks beginning at the reading readiness level and continuing through the sixth or eighth grade levels. The approach presents all of the word recognition and comprehension skills. Its major advantage for a corrective reading program is its sequential skill development. A disabled reader should use a basal reader on his instructional reading level and the teacher should present only those reading skills which he has been diagnosed to need. This approach should always be used in combination with other approaches in a corrective reading program.

The language-experience approach uses child-dictated and child-written experience stories and group-dictated experience charts as the basis of reading materials. Its major advantages are that it reflects each child's own unique experiences and uses their own language patterns. Its major limitation is its lack of sequential skill development. This approach is especially useful with older disabled readers and disadvantaged children.

The individualized reading plan is based on the philsophy that each child seeks to read, should select his own reading materials, and should pace his own reading. In individualized reading a child reads materials which he has chosen independently and meets with his teacher two or three times a week in an individual reading conference. He and his teacher keep records of what he has read. The main advantage of this plan is that it creates an interest in reading in the children who are using it, while its major limitation is its lack of sequential skill development. Individualized reading can be used in a corrective reading program to motivate a disabled reader to read more widely and to reinforce his reading skills.

At the present time there are quite a few formal phonics programs on the American market. They all present many phonetic generalizations and present them earlier than do other reading programs. Some of the formal phonics programs are basic, while others are supplementary. They can be a valuable supplement to some disabled readers who have good auditory discrimination.

The initial teaching alphabet is a medium of teaching beginning reading using forty-four symbols to represent the forty-four sounds found in the English language. It may be valuable in the corrective reading program for a disabled reader who has not learned to read by another method. The diacritical marking system also is an attempt to modify the English language.

There are really two linguistic approaches. The approach of the phonologists uses spelling patterns and a consistent sound-symbol relationship to teach beginning reading. The structuralists do not have reading materials at the present time, but they would use sentence patterns in the teaching of reading. Several materials representing the approach of the phonologists can be helpful for disabled readers who have good auditory discrimination.

Words in Color is a supplementary approach that can be used to teach phonetic analysis. It does this by using color clues to teach sound-symbol relationships. It may be of value to disabled readers who need special help in phonetic analysis and are not color blind. Programmed reading materials are self-instructional and can be used to teach or review certain reading skills, most often the word recognition skills. They can be of use in a corrective reading program especially with slow-learning or disadvantaged children.

Delacato has stated that a prime cause of reading disability is incompletely developed dominance of one side of the brain. He recommends a program with disabled readers to correct this, including cross-pattern creeping, crawling, and walking. Most reading specialists are not convinced of the value of this program at the present time.

There are several methods of grouping elementary children for reading instruction. This chapter described reading achievement groups, needs or skills groups, interest and research groups, the Joplin Plan, and the tutorial system.

REFERENCES

Beery, Althea, Thomas C. Barrett, and William R. Powel. *Elementary Reading Instruction.* Boston: Allyn and Bacon, Incorporated, 1969. Chapters 10 and 4.

Dechant, Emerald V. *Diagnosis and Remediation of Reading Disability.* West Nyack, New York: Parker Publishing Company, Incorporated, 1968. Chapter 5.

Howes, Virgil M. *Individualized Instruction in Reading and Social Studies.* New York: The Macmillan Company, 1970.

Miller, Wilma H. *The First R: Elementary Reading Today.* New York: Holt, Rinehart and Winston, Incorporated, 1972. Chapters 4, 5, 6, 8, 9, and 10.

Spache, George D. and Evelyn B. Spache. *Reading in the Elementary School.* Boston: Allyn and Bacon, Incorporated, 1969. Chapters 3, 4, 5, 6, and 11.

9

How to Gain the Parents' Support in the Prevention and Correction of Reading Difficulties

This chapter is designed for teachers to use in working with the parents of preschool children and disabled readers. It also is written for parents who want to know some ways of helping their preschool children get ready for primary-grade reading and for parents who want to help their child who is disabled in reading achieve the best success possible from a reading improvement program.

In this chapter are illustrated some elements of the home environment which are most related to the later reading success of preschool children. A number of things that parents can do to reinforce either a corrective or remedial reading program such as reading to their child, letting him read along with them, letting him read to them, and providing him with appropriate reading materials.

Home Factors and Later Reading Success

A number of research studies and the writer's experiences suggest many things which can be done in the homes of preschool children to best help them achieve later success in primary-grade reading. The following suggestions can be given to mothers of preschool children no matter what type of reading program these children later may have in the primary grades.

The language spoken by the parents and older brothers and sisters can greatly influence the language spoken by the child which in turn usually helps him in beginning reading activities. The language spoken by the mother probably is the most important since the child usually has the most contact with his mother during the preschool years. It is important for her to try to use complex sentences with many descriptive adjectives and adverbs. She also should use precise vocabulary words and try if possible to relate any new vocabulary words to the objects that they stand for. Of course, the mother should also try to use correct grammar.

All members of the family, but probably the mother in particular, should listen to what the child says and try to take the time to talk directly to him. As much as possible, any questions he asks should be answered correctly and completely so that he will want to keep on asking questions.

In making rules for a child, it normally is important for the parents to give him the reasons for family rules instead of just expecting passive obedience from him since this passive attitude may carry over into his school experiences. It often may be helpful to allow the child to make his views known in some of the family decisions which directly relate to him.

When a mother teaches her child how to do some common job in the home, she should usually try to explain this task to the child fairly specifically before he does it and to give him praise and encouragement as he tries to complete it.

Home prereading activities such as reading to the child, providing him with appropriate reading materials to develop his interest in reading, helping him in an informal way to learn the names and sounds of letters, and helping him to learn a few words by sight undoubtedly are very helpful to his later success in reading. Taking the child on family trips and discussing them may prove to be very useful in helping him to develop the background of experiences that he will need to interpret the materials who he finds in primary-grade reading instruction. Providing the child with manipulative materials such as crayons, drawing paper, paints, and scissors may help him to develop the motor coordination which is related to success in beginning reading.

Although a family does provide its children with the various elements that are related to primary-grade reading achievement, this will not, of course, insure that they will experience success in primary-grade reading. However, it may well help them to experience success with beginning reading activities.

The Home Environment and Reading Success

As a child progresses to the intermediate grades, many of these same elements provided in the home still may influence reading success. Parents can continue to encourage their children to ask questions about words, and they should answer these questions with real interest. Parents who read frequently themselves and really enjoy reading provide a good model for their children in seeing the value and importance of reading.

Providing the child with much appropriate reading materials, mainly on the child's independent reading level or the level at which he can easily read for himself, will motivate him to improve his reading skills and to see the value of good reading ability. Sometimes children need a parent's guidance in choosing material that they can read and in which they have an interest. Asking the child to read several paragraphs of the book aloud near the center of the book provides a good test of the child's ability to read it effectively. Providing the child a place at home where he can read without too many distractions also can be important. Most children, even if they are very good readers, enjoy showing their parents how well they read by reading orally at home to them.

Gaining the Parents' Support in a Reading Improvement Program

The parents of a disabled reader who is receiving corrective or remedial reading instruction often wonder exactly what their role should be in the reading improvement program and how they can best help to reinforce it.

Certainly the first thing that the parents of a disabled reader in a reading improvement program should do is remove pressure from him while he is trying to improve his reading. This is often difficult for parents to do since they usually feel that they have failed as parents in some way if their child has reading difficulties.

Sometimes parents pressure their child to learn to read in a very direct way while at other times the pressure is much more subtle. In either case, a disabled reader can very easily sense the pressure from his parents about his lack of reading ability, and he may feel much more threatened by the reading improvement program than he otherwise would be. Probably parents should tell their child that they really believe that he can and he will make good progress in the reading program and then not spend much more time discussing it.

Obviously, the parents of a disabled reader should *not* try to teach him to read by any kind of formal program. There are on the market today several different formal phonics programs which are designed for parents to use with disabled readers. They cannot be recommended under any circumstances. First, parents are not trained to teach a formal phonics method, and their child may not have the necessary auditory discrimination ability (the ability to hear likenesses and differences in sounds) nor the minimum mental age to succeed in such a program. An exposure to such a formal phonics program can do the child untold harm since he may have to unlearn many concepts as well as overcome an emotional block that he may receive from failing at it.

However, the parents of a disabled reader can answer their child's questions about the names and sounds of letters and about different words and their meanings. This really is the teaching of reading very informally and may help the child without doing him any harm.

To help reinforce a reading improvement program, the parent can ask either the classroom teacher or the special reading teacher if there are some word recognition or comprehension skills which she has taught that the child can now review at home. Often a parent can review some of the reading skills, especially the word recognition skills, at home that were taught to the child by the teacher. Such a review can take the form of the child's dictating a language-experience story, playing a commercially prepared or homemade reading or phonics game, or using flash cards to learn the various sight words. Such a review at home not only can help a disabled reader to retain some of the reading skills which he has learned from his teacher but also can show him that his parents are interested in his reading improvement and want to help him with it. Most parents are very willing to reinforce the reading skills that have been taught to their child if they know *exactly* how to do it and are convinced that they are not doing him any harm. In this way they also get the feeling that they are doing something concrete to help their child improve his reading.

Parents also can help to reinforce a reading improvement program by spending time reading stories and books to their child which are several years in advance of the child's actual reading level but are in the range of his interests.

Parents also can choose a book that the child can easily read and one that interests him. The parents or an older brother or sister can then begin to read the story to the child, and the child takes turns with the family member in reading the story out loud. Sometimes the family member reads one line and the child the next, and sometimes the parent reads one paragraph and the child reads the next one. Reading aloud with the family member provides a good motivation for the disabled reader as well as helping him to learn to follow along effectively and to share a rewarding experience with reading.

Disabled readers also can receive much motivation in reinforcing a reading improvement program by reading aloud to the family members. Such oral reading may be done from language-experience stories which the child has dictated or written, from children's magazines or newspapers, and from tradebooks (library books) which the parents have purchased for their child, or have checked out for him from a public or school library. It probably is important for a disabled reader to own a few of his own books which he can reread many times and which really belong to him. It is very important that each book interests the child and is on his independent or free reading level. This is especially important because a disabled reader always needs to experience complete success with his reading and to develop fluency in both his silent and oral reading. The independent or free reading level usually is about one and one-half to two years below a child's instructional grade level or the reading level at which he receives actual reading instruction. A list of some high-interest and low-vocabulary books which a parent may want to get for his child to read is found in Appendix VIII.

When a disabled reader is reading orally to a family member, the parent should give as much praise and encouragement as possible and refrain from putting too much pressure on him for perfection in reading. As much as possible, it is important for the oral reading to take place in a permissive atmosphere which is free from strain for the child. When the child comes to a word that he does not know (which should not happen very often since each book should be very easy for the child to read), the parent can supply the unknown word without trying to teach it to the child, by using phonetic analysis. The parents can ask a few simple comprehension questions after the child has read the story or the book orally to be sure that he has really understood it.

The First Parent-Teacher Interview

Interviews between the parents of disabled readers and teachers in either a corrective or remedial reading program can be very important in helping the disabled reader to succeed in the program. This section of the chapter is designed to give the reader only a brief but helpful overview of the interview technique.

The parent (usually the mother) often is asked to meet with the reading teacher toward the beginning of a reading improvement program to help the parent and teacher get assistance and understanding from each other. When the parent does come for the first interview, it is very important that the reading teacher make a special effort to establish rapport with her and put her completely at ease. This is the teacher's responsibility since the interview takes place at school which is the special domain of the teacher.

It usually is important for the teacher to listen and try to understand the mother as much as possible rather than to direct the interview in a structured way especially if the mother is willing and able to talk quite freely. The teacher can ask the mother to tell her what she thinks the child's reading problem may be and what the causes for it are. A parent often is able to tell the teacher a great deal about the child's reading difficulties if she is asked. The teacher must be very willing to listen and to consider carefully what has been said. During the interview the teacher can find out something about the family's educational attainment, occupational status, and socio-economic class if this is done in a *very non-threatening way*. The teacher has to exercise great tact and care during this part of the interview. The mother may also be able to give the teacher helpful information about the child's early development at home and his first experiences with reading at school.

The teacher has an obligation to the parent during the first interview. The parent can expect that the reading teacher will explain a little about some of the various methods of teaching reading in a way that the parent can find easy to understand. The teacher also can tell the mother some of the various ways that she will use to find out about the child's reading problems and his reading level. She also can talk about what she may then plan to do for the child after the diagnosis. She can explain that the diagnosis will include the giving of some standardized and informal reading tests and talking with and observing the child. The teacher should be realistic with the mother about the child's chances for reading improvement, but she can assure the mother that with proper reading instructions fitted to the child's interests, reading level, and reading needs, the chances are excellent that he will make very good improvement in the reading program.

All through any reading improvement program, it is extremely important that the parent and reading teacher maintain a friendly relationship with mutual respect, understanding, and reinforcement of the program.

SUMMARY

This chapter discussed some elements of the home environment which are most related to the school reading success of preschool children, and told parents how to provide these elements in the home. The language spoken by the members of the family, especially by the mother, is very important since a preschool child learns to speak through imitation. The mother's language should contain complex sentences, precise vocabulary, and correct grammar. Parents should listen to their child and answer his questions, and provide a number of prereading experiences in the home such as reading to him, taking him on family trips, answering his questions about letters and words, and giving him materials to work with.

Many of these same elements of the home environment continue to influence reading success in the elementary school for all children. Parents of a disabled reader can do a number of things which will help to reinforce a reading improvement program. Undue pressure to succeed in reading should be removed by the parents, and they should not try to teach their child to read by any kind of formal program. However, parents can often reinforce the reading skills taught in the reading improvement program in a number of ways. They can read aloud to the child, let him read aloud with them, and let him read aloud to them. The parent can ask the disabled reader some comprehension questions after he has read a story or a book aloud to them.

The first parent-teacher interview can be a great help in the understanding of the disabled reader and his reading problem. The teacher can often learn much about the child and his reading difficulties if she is very tactful in talking to the mother. The teacher can explain some aspects of reading instruction and something about the reading improvement program.

REFERENCES

Carter, Homer L. G. and Dorothy J. McGinnis. *Diagnosis and Treatment of the Disabled Reader.* New York: The Macmillan Company, 1970. Chapter 6. Chapter 16 (pp. 297-300).

Miller, Wilma H. "Home Prereading Experiences and First-Grade Reading Achievement," *The Reading Teacher,* Volume 22, April, 1969, pp. 641-645.

Miller, Wilma H. "When Mothers Teach Their Children," *The Elementary School Journal,* Volume 70, October, 1969, pp. 38-42.

Strang, Ruth. *Diagnostic Teaching of Reading.* New York: McGraw-Hill Book Company, 1969. Chapter 12.

Wilson, Robert M. *Diagnostic and Remedial Teaching for Classroom and Clinic.* Columbus, Ohio: Charles E. Merrill Books, Incorporated, 1967. Chapter 10.

Zintz, Miles V. *Corrective Reading.* Dubuque, Iowa: William C. Brown Company, Publishers, 1966. Chapter 8.

APPENDIX I

Individual and Group Intelligence Tests

Revised Stanford-Binet Intelligence Scale: Third Edition
Available From Houghton Mifflin Company

This is a test of general intelligence which is individually given to children from age two on through the adult level. It stresses verbal intelligence and yields mental age score. It should be given by someone trained in its administration.

Wechsler Intelligence Scale for Children (WISC)
Available from the Psychological Corporation

This in an individual intelligence test which can be given to children from ages five through fifteen. It contains five verbal tests and five performance tests. It yields a verbal IQ, a performance IQ, and a full scale IQ. Individual subtests have been found to be predictive of reading disability. It should be given by someone trained in its administration.

Arthur Point Scale of Performance
Available from the Psychological Corporation

This test is individually administered and it does not test language ability. Therefore, it is good for bilingual, deaf, and speech defective children. It can be used with children from five to fifteen years of age. It contains five non-language subtests.

California Test of Mental Maturity, 1963 Revision
Available from California Test Bureau

This short-form group intelligence test has eight levels from kindergarten through the college level. It provides separate and total language and nonlanguage mental ages and intelligence quotients. It is also available in a long form.

I. P. A. T. Culture Fair Inteligence Tests
Available from the Bobbs-Merrill Company

This test can be used with children eight years of age through secondary school level. It gives a measure of intelligence and its scores are not much influenced by educational or experiential background. Therefore, it is valuable with culturally disadvantaged children.

Kuhlmann-Anderson IQ Test
Available from the Bobbs-Merrill Company

This test is designed for students in grades kindergarten through twelve and there are tests for each grade level. The tests below the fifth-grade level do not include much reading. The tests measure general intelligence.

Lorge-Thorndike Intelligence Tests
Available from the Houghton Mifflin Company

This test can be used in grades three through twelve. The materials for all grades are found in one booklet which contains eight levels of difficulty. It provides verbal, nonverbal, and total scores.

Otis Quick-Scoring Mental Ability Tests
Available from Harcourt, Brace and World, Incorporated

The Alpha Short Form is used in grades one through four. This is a group intelligence test which requires no reading. The Beta Test is used in grades four through nine, and the Gamma Test is used at the high school and college levels. Each level has Forms Em and Fm.

Peabody Picture Vocabulary Test
Available from the American Guidance Service, Incorporated

This is an individually administered test of verbal intelligence and requires no reading. Therefore, it is very useful in a corrective reading program. It also is easy to administer and score and is valid.

Pintner-Cunningham Primary Test
Available from Harcourt, Brace and World, Incorporated

This is a group intelligence test requiring no reading which can be given to children from kindergarten through grade two. It is available in Forms A and B.

SRA Primary Mental Abilities Test
Available from Science Research Associates

This test provides separate mental ages and intelligence quotients for verbal meaning, number facility, reasoning, perceptual speed, and spatial relation as well as a total score. The test has five levels.

APPENDIX II

Reading Readiness Tests

American School Reading Readiness Test: Revised Edition
Available from the Bobbs-Merrill Company

This test can be given in late kindergarten or beginning first grade and is a group test. It measures vocabulary, discrimination of letter forms, discrimination of words by selection and matching, recognition of geometric forms, following directions, and memory of geometric forms. It is available in Form X.

Gates-MacGinitie Reading Readiness Test
Available from the Teachers College Press, Columbia University

This is a group and individual test to be given at the end of kindergarten or beginning of first grade. It contains the subtests of listening comprehension, auditory discrimination, visual discrimination, following directions, letter recognition, visual-motor coordination, and auditory blending. A word recognition test is included to locate early readers.

Harrison-Stroud Reading Readiness Profiles
Available from the Houghton Mifflin Company

This test can be used in late kindergarten or early first grade and contains the subtests of ability to use symbols, visual discrimination, use of context, auditory discrimination, and letter naming.

Lee-Clark Reading Readiness Tests
Available from the California Test Bureau

This test can be used in late kindergarten or early first grade and is a group test. It contains the subtests of visual discrimination of letter symbols and word shapes. It also measures a child's knowledge of vocabulary and concepts.

Lippincott Reading Readiness Test
Available from Lyons and Carnahan Company

This test can be given the last half of kindergarten or the first part of first grade. It is a group test and measures each child's knowledge of printed, spoken, and written letter forms. The second part of the test contains a readiness checklist.

The Metropolitan Readiness Tests
Available from Harcourt, Brace and World, Incorporated

This group test is designed for use at the late kindergarten or early first grade level. It measures word meaning, sentence meaning, information, matching, numbers, and copying. A supplementary test asks the child to draw a man.

Monroe Reading Aptitude Test
Available from Houghton Mifflin Company

This test is partly group administered and partly individually administered. It can be given from beginning grade one and to nonreaders nine years of age. It tests visual discrimination, auditory discrimination, motor control, oral speed and articulation, and language.

Murphy-Durrell Reading Readiness Analysis
Available from Harcourt, Brace and World, Incorporated

This test is a group test and can be given the last part of kindergarten or the first part of first grade. It tests identifying separate sounds in spoken words, identifying capital and lower-case letters pronounced by the examiner, and learning rate by recognizing some sight words an hour after the examiner taught them.

Steinbach Test of Reading Readiness
Available from Scholastic Testing Service Incorporated

This test can be given the last part of kindergarten or the first part of first grade and is group administered. It tests letter identification, word identification, ability to follow directions, and ability to relate words and pictures.

APPENDIX III

Survey Reading Tests

American School Achievement Tests
Available from the Bobbs-Merrill Company

There are four batteries for use in grades one through nine. The various batteries test word recognition, word meaning, sentence meaning, and paragraph meaning.

Botel Reading Inventory
Available from the Follett Educational Corporation

This test is a group of tests for determining instructional reading levels. It can be used in grades one through twelve and measures word recognition, listening comprehension and phonics.

California Reading Tests, WXYZ Series
Available from the California Test Bureau

There are five batteries in this test for use in grades one through college. Each test has two main areas: vocabulary and comprehension. There are two to four forms at each level.

Gates-MacGinitie Reading Tests
Available from Teachers College Press, Columbia University

There are six forms for use in grades one through nine. Generally, these tests measure vocabulary and comprehension and speed and accuracy. The tests are available in Forms one, two, and three.

Iowa Silent Reading Tests: New Edition
Available from Harcourt, Brace and World, Incorporated

This test contains an elementary battery for grades four through eight. It tests silent reading in the areas of sentence meaning, paragraph meaning, vocabulary, rate, and comprehension. It is available in Forms Am, Bm, Cm, and Dm.

Lee-Clark Reading Tests: 1963 Revision
Available from the California Test Bureau

These tests are designed for use in grades kindergarten through two. They measure reading readiness and reading achievement.

Metropolitan Reading Tests
Available from Harcourt, Brace and World, Incorporated

These tests are found in five batteries and can be used from the end of first grade through eighth grade. In general, the tests measure word knowledge, word discrimination, and paragraph comprehension. They are available in Forms A and B.

Sequential Tests of Educational Progress: Reading
Available from the Educational Testing Service

This test contains four levels for grades four through college. It tests ability to recall ideas, make inferences, sense the author's mood, analyze presentation, and criticize.

Stanford Reading Tests: 1964 Revision
Available from Harcourt, Brace and World, Incorporated

This test has five batteries for grades 1.5 through 9.9. The various tests measure word reading, word meaning, paragraph meaning, and word-study skills. Each level is available in Forms W, X, and Y.

Wide Range Achievement Test: Revised Edition
Available from The Psychological Corporation

This test can be used from age five through adulthood. It is an individual test of word recognition, spelling, and arithmetic computation.

APPENDIX IV

Diagnostic Reading Tests

Bond-Clymer-Hoyt Silent Reading Test (Developmental Reading Test)
Available from Lyons and Carnahan and Company

This test is designed to use in grades three through eight. This diagnostic reading test is given in a group setting and it is made up of eleven subtests. These subtests are recognition of words in isolation, recognition of words in context, recognition of reversible words in context, location of parts of words useful in word recognition, syllabication, locating root words, phonetic knowledge—general word elements, recognition of beginning sounds, selecting rhyming words, identification of letter sounds, and ability to blend phonetically and visually.

Diagnostic Reading Tests
Available from the Committee on Diagnostic Reading Tests

This is a series of survey and diagnostic tests designed for use in grades one through college level. Generally the diagnostic tests are given to those students who do poorly on the survey tests. They test word recognition, vocabulary, comprehension, story reading, story comprehension, and rate of comprehension at the highest battery. The tests are composed of three batteries designed for use in grades one-four, grades four-eight, and grades seven-sixteen. The tests are available in Forms A and B.

Doren Diagnostic Reading Test
Available from American Guidance Service, Incorporated

This is a group test designed for use in grades two through eight. It tests word recognition skills in detail. It is composed of the subtests of beginning sounds, sight words, rhyming, whole-word recognition, words within words, speech consonants, blending, vowels, ending sounds, discriminate guessing, and letter recognition.

Durrell Analysis of Reading Difficulty: New Edition
Available from Harcourt, Brace and World, Incorporated

This is an individual test designed for use in grades one through six. The checklist of errors which accompanies it probably is the best of its kind. It is made up of the subtests of oral reading test, silent reading test, listening comprehension test, word recognition and word analysis test, naming letters, identifying letter names, matching letters, writing letters, visual memory of words, hearing sounds in words, learning to hear sounds in words, learning rate, phonic spelling of words, spelling tests, and handwriting tests. It also includes a set of reading paragraphs, word lists, and a cardboard tachistoscope.

Gates-McKillop Diagnostic Tests
Available from Teachers College Press, Columbia University

This test is designed for use in grades one through eight. It is an individual test and is quite difficult to administer and to score. Therefore, it should mainly be used with severely disabled readers. It tests oral reading, word perception, phrase perception, blending word parts, giving letter sounds, naming letters, recognizing visual form of sounds, auditory blending, spelling, oral vocabulary, syllabication, and auditory discrimination. It is available in Forms 1 and 2.

McCullough Word Analysis Tests
Available from Ginn and Company

This test can be used in grades four through six and it is a group test of word recognition skills. It tests initial consonant blends and digraphs, comparing vowel sounds, matching symbols with vowel sounds, identifying phonetic respellings, using a pronunciation key, dividing between syllables, and finding a root word.

Spache Diagnostic Reading Scales
Available from California Test Bureau

This test is designed for use in grades one through eight. It is an individually administered test and can be used at the secondary school level with disabled readers. It consists of three word lists, twenty-two graded reading passages, and six supplementary phonics tests. Each pupil is given three reading levels: the instructional level in oral reading, the independent level in silent reading, and the potential level in listening comprehension.

Stanford Diagnostic Reading Test
Available from Harcourt, Brace and World, Incorporated

This test has two levels–Level I designed for use in grades 2.5-4.5 and Level II designed for use in grades 4.5-8.5. It is a group test with subtests of comprehension, vocabulary, syllabication, auditory skills, phonetic analysis, and rate of reading.

APPENDIX V

Oral Reading Tests

Gilmore Oral Reading Test, New Edition
Available from Harcourt, Brace and World

This test is designed for grades one through eight. It is an individual reading test of oral reading ability including ten oral reading paragraphs of increasing difficulty based on one theme. It is scored for accuracy, comprehension, and rate of oral reading. It is available in Forms C and D.

Gray Oral Reading Tests
Available from the Bobbs-Merrill Company

This test can be given individually in grades one—ten. It has thirteen graded oral reading paragraphs in each form. It tests the accuracy and rate of oral reading combined in a composite score. It is available in Forms A, B, C, and D.

Leavell Analytical Oral Reading Test
Available from the American Guidance Service, Incorporated

This test is designed for use in grades one-ten. It is given individually, and the graded oral reading paragraphs make up one continuous story. It measures oral reading ability in terms of comprehension, accuracy, and rate.

APPENDIX VI

Phonetic Generalizations

1. The consonants usually are represented by only one sound. However, the consonant "c" has no sound of its own, but borrows the sound "k" as in the word "can" or the sound of "s" as in the word "ceiling." The consonant "g" also has the sounds illustrated in the words "gate" and "gem." The consonant "s" has the sounds as illustrated in the words "see" and "rose." The consonant "q" borrows the sounds of the consonants "kw" as in the word "quick," and the consonant "x" borrows the sounds of "ks" as in the word "example."

2. The vowels all are represented by several different sounds.

3. Long vowel sounds usually are identified as the names of the letters themselves. As an example, the letter names of "a," "e," "i," "o," and "u." However, the vowel "u" also can have the sound which it does in the word "jūice."

4. A single vowel followed by a consonant in a word or syllable often has the short sound. As an example, "măn" or "pĕncĭl."

5. When two vowels are found together, the first one often has the long sound, while the second one often is silent. As an example, "bōat" or "tīe."

6. In words which contain two vowels, one of which is final "e," the first vowel is long and the final "e" often is silent. As an example, "rōpe" or "bāke."

7. A single vowel that ends a word or syllable usually has the long sound. As an example, "shē," "tā/ble," or "lō/cō/mō/tĭve."

8. The digraphs "ew," "au," "oo," form a single sound that is not the long sound of the first vowel. As an example, "new," "maul," and "book" and "noon."

9. The vowel "a" followed by an "l" or "w" usually results in a blended sound. As an example, "ball," "hall," "paw," or "saw."

10. Single vowels followed by an "r" usually result in a blended sound. As an example, "turn," "herd," "skirt," "far," or "car."

11. The consonant "w" usually changes the sound of the vowels which follow it. As an example, "warm," "world," or "worm."

12. The letter "y" at the end of a word containing no other vowel usually has the long sound of "i." As an example, "flȳ," "mȳ," or "trȳ."

13. Diphthongs are two-vowel combinations in which two vowels contribute to the speech sound. As an example, "toy," "how," or "mouse."

14. A consonant blend is two or three adjacent consonants which are blended together when they are pronounced. As an example, "blew," "drink," "splash," or "string."

15. A consonant digraph is composed of two consonants in which both consonants contribute to the speech sound. As an example, "which," "ship," "the," "thin," or "ring."

16. The finding of little words in big words often is of questionable value. As an example, it is not accurate in the words "father" or "mother."

17. Some consonants are silent. As an example, "write," "sigh," "knee," or "gnaw."

APPENDIX VII

Structural and Accent Generalizations

1. Each syllable must contain at least one vowel. When two consonants come between vowels, usually one consonant goes with each vowel. As an example, "but/ter," "bas/ket," or "can/dy."

2. When one consonant comes between two vowels, the first syllable usually ends with the vowel and the second syllable usually begins with the second consonant. The syllable ending with the vowel sound usually has a long vowel sound. As an example, "ta/ble," "ti/ger," "to/tal," or "hu/mor."

3. When the first of two vowels separated by a single consonant has a short sound, the single intervening consonant ends the first syllable. As an example, "cam/el," or "mag/a/zine."

4. A compound word is divided between the two small words which compose it. As an example, "police/man," "cow/boy," or "play/ground."

5. Suffixes which begin with a vowel usually are separate syllables. This is not true of "ed", except when it is preceded by "t" or "d." As an example, "cook/ing," "tell/ing," or "want/ed."

6. Prefixes usually form a separate syllable when they are added to a word. As an example, "un/happy," "mis/spell," "dis/like."

7. Certain letter combinations at the end of words form a final syllable. As an example, "puz/zle," "ta/ble," "dim/ple," "gen/tle," "un/cle," "strug/gle," "can/dle," or "wrin/kle."

8. Most words of one syllable remain intact as syllables when a suffix is added. As an example, "tell/ing," "need/ed," or "spell/ing."

9. The first syllable is usually accented in a word of only two syllables. As an example, "ta' ble," "ba' sic," "to' tal," or "den' tist."

10. The first syllable is usually accented in words of two syllables unless

the second syllable contains two vowels and then it is accented. As an example, "re ceive'," "par rade'," or "ap point'."

11. A compound word usually is accented on the first syllable. As an example, "cow' girl," "fire' man," "pass' port."

12. Words of three syllables usually are accented on the first or second syllable. As an example, "e las' tic," "ma ter· nal," "oc' cu py," or "scen' er y."

13. Words of four or more syllables usually have both a primary and a secondary accent. As an example, "tel' e vi' sion," "con' cen tra' tion," "rem' i nis' cence," or "in' ap proach' a ble."

14. Primary accent sometimes shifts when the suffix is added to a root word. As an example, "sep' a rate" becomes "sep a ra' tion."

APPENDIX VIII

High-Interest, Low-Vocabulary Books

TITLE	*Reading Grade Level*	*Interest Grade Level*	*Publisher*
Beginner Books	1	1-4	Random House
Basic Vocabulary Series	1-3	2-4	Garrard Press
Cowboy Sam Books	1-3	1-4	Benefic Press
Sailor Jack Books	1-3	2-6	Benefic Press
Dan Frontier Books	1-3	2-7	Benefic Press
Checkered Flag Series	2	6-12	Field Enterprises
Jim Forest Readers	2-3	3-6	Field Enterprises
Gateway Books	2-3	3-8	Random House
The True Books	2-3	2-6	Children's Press
All About Books Series	2-4	2-6	Children's Press
The Deep Sea Adventure Series	2-4	3-8	Field Enterprises
The Morgan Bay Series	2-4	4-8	Field Enterprises
The Wildlife Adventure Series	2-4	3-8	Field Enterprises
American Adventure Series	3-6	4-8	Harper and Row
Frontiers of America Series	3-4	3-8	Children's Press
Pleasure Reading Series	3-4	3-6	The Garrard Press
Americans All Series	4-5	4-8	Field Enterprises
Pioneer Series	4-5	4-8	Benefic Press
Childhood of Famous American Series	4-5	4-8	The Bobbs-Merrill Co.
Teen-Age Tales	4-6	6-10	D.C. Heath Company
Simplified Classics	4-5	4-8	Scott Foresman
Modern Adventure Stories	4-6	4-10	Harper and Row
Landmark Books	5-6	5-10	Random House
World Landmark Books	5-6	5-10	Random House
All About Books	5-6	5-10	Random House

APPENDIX IX

Professional Books on Reading

The following list of professional books for the teacher of reading obviously is only a selection of all the possible titles which could be included. However, the list includes many of the recent useful books in the area.

Austin, Mary C. et. al. *The Torch Lighters: Tomorrow's Teachers of Reading.* Cambridge: Harvard University Press, 1961.

Bagford, Jack. *Phonics: Its Role in Teaching Reading.* Iowa City: Sernoll, Incorporated, 1961.

Barbe, Walter B. *Educator's Guide to Personalized Reading Instruction.* Englewood Cliffs, New Jersey: Prentice-Hall, 1961.

Beery, Althea, Thomas C. Barrett, and William R. Powell. *Elementary Reading Instruction.* Boston: Allyn and Bacon, Incorporated, 1969.

Bloomfield, Leonard and Clarence L. Barnhart. *Let's Read.* Detroit: Wayne State University Press, 1961.

Bond, Guy L. and Miles A. Tinker. *Reading Difficulties: Their Diagnosis and Correction.* New York: Appleton-Century-Crofts, 1967.

Bond, Guy L. and Eva Bond Wagner. *Teaching the Child to Read.* New York: The Macmillan Company, 1966.

Brogan, Peggy and Lorene K. Fox. *Helping Children Read.* New York: Holt, Rinehart and Winston, Incorporated, 1961.

Bush, Clifford L. and Mildred H. Huebner, *Strategies for Reading in the Elementary School.* New York: The Macmillan Company, 1970.

Cheyney, Arnold B. *Teaching Culturally Disadvantaged in the Elementary School.* Columbus, Ohio: Charles E. Merrill Books, 1967.

Carter, Homer L. J. and Dorothy J. McGinnis. *Diagnosis and Treatment of the Disabled Reader.* New York: The Macmillan Company, 1970.

Cordts, Anna D. *Phonics For the Reading Teacher.* New York: Holt, Rinehart and Winston, Incorporated, 1965.

Cushenberry, Donald C. *Reading Improvement in the Elementary School.* West Nyack, N.Y.: Parker Publishing Company, Inc., 1969.

Darrow, Helen F. and Virgil M. Howes. *Approaches to Individualized Reading.* New York: Appleton-Century-Crofts, 1960.

Dechant, Emerald V. *Diagnosis and Remediation of Reading Disability.* West Nyack, New York: Parker Publishing Company, 1968.

Dechant, Emerald V. *Improving the Teaching of Reading.* Englewood Cliffs, New Jersey: Prentice-Hall 1970.

Delacato, Carl H. *The Diagnosis and Treatment of Speech and Reading Problems.* Springfield, Illinois: Charles C. Thomas Publishers, 1963.

Durkin, Dolores. *Phonics and the Teaching of Reading.* New York: Bureau of Publications, Teachers College Press, Columbia University, 1962.

Durkin, Dolores. *Teaching Them All to Read.* Boston, Allyn and Bacon, Incorporated, 1970.

Farr, Roger. *Measurement and Evaluation of Reading.* New York: Harcourt, Brace and World, Incorporated, 1970.

Fernald, Grace M. *Remedial Techniques in Basic School Subjects.* New York: McGraw-Hill Book Company, 1966.

Fries, Charles C. *Linguistics and Reading.* New York: Holt, Rinehart and Winston, Incorporated, 1963.

Gans, Roma. *Common Sense in Teaching Reading.* Indianapolis: Bobbs-Merrill Company, Incorporated, 1963.

Gillingham, Anna and Bessie E. Stillman. *Remedial Training for Children With Specific Disability in Reading, Spelling, and Penmanship.* Cambridge: Educators Publishing Service, 1960.

Gray, William S. *On Their Own in Reading.* Chicago: Scott, Forseman and Company, 1960.

Harris, Albert J. *How to Increase Reading Ability.* New York: David McKay Company, 1970.

Heilman, Arthur W. *Phonics in Proper Perspective.* Columbus, Ohio: Charles E. Merrill Books, 1964.

Heilman, Arthur W. *Principles and Practices of Teaching Reading.* Columbus, Ohio: Charles E. Merrill Books, 1967.

Hildreth, Gertrude H. *Teaching Reading.* New York: Holt, Rinehart and Winston, Incorporated, 1958.

Howes, Virgil M. *Individualizing Instruction in Reading and Social Studies.* New York: The Macmillan Company, 1970.

International Reading Association. *Sources of Good Books for Poor Readers.* Newark, Delaware: International Reading Association, 1964.

Kephart, Newell. *The Slow Learner in the Classroom.* Indianapolis: The Bobbs-Merrill Company, 1960.

Kottmeyer, William. *Teacher's Guide for Remedial Reading.* St. Louis: Webster Publishing Company, 1959.

Lefevre, Carl. *Linguistics and the Teaching of Reading.* New York: McGraw-Hill Book Company, 1964.

McKee, Paul and William K. Durr. *Reading: A Program of Instruction for the Elementary School* Boston: Houghton Mifflin Company, 1966.

Miller, Wilma H. *The First R: Elementary Reading Today.* New York: Holt, Rinehart and Winston, Incorporated, 1972.

Miller, Wilma H. *Elementary Reading Today: Selected Articles.* New York: Holt, Rinehart and Winston, Incorporated, 1972.

Monroe, Marion and Bernice Rogers. *Foundations for Reading.* Chicago: Scott, Foresman and Company, 1964.

Otto, Wayne and Richard A. McMenemy. *Corrective and Remedial Teaching.* Boston: Houghton Mifflin Company, 1966.

Robinson, Helen M. *Corrective Reading in Classroom and Clinic.* Chicago: University of Chicago Press, 1958.

Robinson, Helen M. *Why Pupils Fail in Reading.* Chicago: University of Chicago Press, 1946.

Roswell, Florence and Gladys Natchez. *Reading Disability: Diagnosis and Treatment.* New York: Basic Books, 1964.

Smith, Nila Banton. *American Reading Instruction.* Newark, Delaware: International Reading Association, 1965.

Spache, George D. *Good Reading for Poor Readers.* Champaign, Illinois: Garrard Press, 1966.

Spache, George D. and Evelyn B. Spache. *Reading in the Elementary School.* Boston: Allyn and Bacon, Incorporated, 1969.

Strang, Ruth. *Diagnostic Teaching of Reading.* New York: McGraw-Hill Book Company, 1969.

Strang, Ruth. *Reading Diagnosis and Remediation.* Newark, Delaware: IRA Research Fund, 1968.

Strang, Ruth. *Understanding and Helping the Retarded Reader.* Tucson: University of Arizona Press, 1965.

Strang, Ruth, Constance M. McCullough, and Arthur E. Traxler. *The Improvement of Reading.* New York: McGraw-Hill Book Company, 1967.

Tinker, Miles A. and Constance M. McCullough. *Teaching Elementary Reading.* New York: Appleton-Century-Crofts, 1968.

Veatch, Jeannette and Philip J. Acinapuro. *Reading in the Elementary School.* New York: The Ronald Press, 1966.

Wilson, Robert M. *Diagnostic and Remedial Reading.* Columbus, Ohio: Charles E. Merrill Books, 1967.

Woolf, Maurice D. and Jeanne A. Woolf. *Remedial Reading: Teaching and Treatment.* New York: McGraw-Hill Book Company, 1957.

Zintz, Miles V. *Corrective Reading.* Dubuque, Iowa: William C. Brown, Publishers, 1966.

APPENDIX X

List of Book Publishers

Abelard-Schuman, Limited, 6 West 57th Street, New York, New York 10019

Abingdon Press, 201 Eight Avenue, South, Nashville, Tennessee 37203

Allyn and Bacon, Incorporated, 150 Tremont Street, Boston, Massachusetts 02111

American Book Company, 300 Pike Street, Cincinnati, Ohio 45202

American Education Publishers, Incorporated, 55 High Street, Middletown, New York 10003

American Guidance Service, Incorporated, Circle Pines, Minnesota 55014

American Library Association, 50 East Huron Street, Chicago, Illinois 60611

Appleton-Century-Crofts, Incorporated, 440 Park Avenue South, New York, New York 10016

Basic Books, Incorporated, 404 Park Avenue South, New York, New York 10016

Bausch and Lomb Optical Company, Rochester, New York 14602

Beckley-Cardy Company, 1900 North Narragansett Avenue, Chicago, Illinois 60639

Benefic Press Publications, 10300 West Roosevelt Road, Westchester, Illinois 60153

Bobbs-Merrill Comapny, Incorporated, 4300 West 62nd Street, Indianapolis, Ind. 46206

Milton Bradley Company, Springfield, Massachusetts 01101

Burgess Publishing Company, 428 South Sixth Street, Minneapolis, Minnesota 55415

Center for Applied Research in Education, Incorporated, 521 Fifth Avenue, New York, New York 10017

Chandler Publishing Company, 125 Spear Street, San Francisco, California 94105

Children's Press, Incorporated, 1224 West Van Buren Street, Chicago, Illinois 60607

Consulting Psychologists Press, 577 College Avenue, Palo Alto, California 94306

Coronet Films, 65 East South Water Street, Chicago, Illinois 60601

Coward-McCann Incorporated, 200 Madison Avenue, New York, New York 10016

Thomas Y. Crowell Company, 201 Park Avenue South, New York, New York 10003

Dodd, Mead and Company, Incorporated, 79 Madison Avenue, New York, New York 10016

Doubleday and Company, Incorporated, 277 Park Avenue, New York, New York 10017

E. P. Dutton and Company, 201 Park Avenue, New York, New York 10003

Educational Developmental Laboratories, Incorporated, Huntington, New York 11743

Educators Publishing Service, Incorporated, 75 Moulton Street, Cambridge, Massachusetts 02138

Essay Press, Incorporated, P. O. Box 5, Planetarium Station, New York, New York 10024

Fearon Publishers, Incorporated, 2165 Park Boulevard, Palo Alto, California 94306

Field Enterprises Educational Corporation, 510 Merchandise Mart Plaza, Chicago, Illinois 60654

Follett Publishing Company, 1010 West Washington Boulevard, Chicago, Illinois 60607

Garrard Publishing Company, 1607 North Market Street, Champaign, Illinois 61820

Ginn and Company, Waltham, Massachusetts 02154

Golden Press Publishers, 850 Third Avenue, New York, New York 10022

Grossett and Dunlap, 51 Madison Avenue, New York, New York 10010

The Gryphon Press, Highland Park, New Jersey 08904

E. M. Hale and Company, 1201 South Hastings Way, Eau Claire, Wisconsin 54701

Harper and Row Publishers, Incorporated, 49 East 33rd Street, New York, New York 10016

D. C. Heath and Company, 285 Columbus Avenue, Boston, Massachusetts 02116

Holt, Rinehart and Winston, Incorporated, 383 Madison Avenue, New York, New York 10017

Houghton Mifflin Company, 2 Park Street, Boston, Massachusetts, 02107

Initial Teaching Alphabet Publications, Incorporated, 20 East 46th Street, New York, New York 10017

International Reading Association, 6 Tyre Avenue, Newark, Delaware 19711

Keystone View Company, Meadville, Pennsylvania 16335

Alfred A. Knopf, 825 Third Avenue, New York, New York 10017

J. B. Lippincott Company, East Washington Square, Philadelphia, Pennsylvania 19105

Lyons and Carnahan, Incorporated, 307 East 25th Street, Chicago, Illinois 60616

McCormick-Mathers Publishing Company, Incorporated, P. O. Box 2212, Wichita, Kansas 67201

McGraw-Hill Book Company, 330 West 42nd Street, New York, New York 10036

David McKay Company, Incorporated, 750 Third Avenue, New York, New York 10017

The Macmillan Company, 866 Third Avenue, New York, New York 10022

Charles E. Merrill Books, Incorporated, 1300 Alum Creek Drive, Columbus, Ohio 43216

William Morrow and Company, Incorporated, 425 Park Avenue South, New York, New York 10016

National Council of Teachers of English, 508 South Sixth Street, Champaign, Illinois 61820

Noble and Noble, Publishers, 750 Third Avenue, New York, New York 10017

F. A. Owen Publishing Company, 7 Bank Street, Dansville, New York 14437

Parker Publishing Company, Incorporated, West Nyack, New York 10994

Prentice-Hall, Incorporated, Englewood Cliffs, New Jersey 07632

The Psychological Corporation, 304 East 45th Street, New York, New York 10017

G. P. Putnam's Sons, 200 Madison Avenue, New York, New York 10016

Rand-McNally and Company, P. O. Box 7600, Chicago, Illinois 60680

Random House, 457 Madison Avenue, New York, New York 10022

Readers Digest, Educational Division, Pleasantville, New York 10570

Henry Regnery Company, 114 West Illinois Street, Chicago, Illinois 60610

The Ronald Press Company, 79 Madison Avenue, New York, New York 10016

Science Research Associates, Incorporated, 259 East Erie Street, Chicago, Illinois 60611

Scott, Foresman and Company, 1900 East Lake Avenue, Glenview, Illinois 60025

Charles Scribner's Sons, 597 Fifth Avenue, New York, New York 10017

Silver Burdett Company, Park Avenue and Columbus Road, Morristown, New Jersey 07960

Simon and Schuster, Incorporated, 1 West 39th Street, New York, New York 10018

Steck-Vaughn Company, P. O. Box 2028, Austin, Texas 78767

Teachers College Press, Columbia University, 525 West 120th Street, New York, New York 10027

Charles C. Thomas Publishers, 301 E. Lawrence Avenue, Springfield, Illinois 62703

University of Chicago Press, 5750 Ellis Avenue, Chicago, Illinois 60637

Harvard University Press, 79 Garden Street, Cambridge, Massachusetts 02138

University of Iowa Press, Iowa City, Iowa 52240

The Viking Press, Incorporated, 625 Madison Avenue, New York, New York 10022

Webster Division of McGraw-Hill Book Company, Manchester Road, Manchester, Missouri 63062

Albert Whitman and Company, 560 West Lake Street, Chicago, Illinois 60606

H. W. Wilson Company, 950 University Avenue, Bronx, New York 10452

Winterhaven Lions Research Foundation, Incorporated, Box 122, Winter Haven, Florida 33880

Xerox Corporation, Curriculum Programs, 600 Madison Avenue, New York, New York 10022

APPENDIX XI

Test Publishers

American Guidance Service, Incorporated, Circle Pines, Minnesota 55014

The Bobbs-Merrill Publishing Company, Incorporated, 4300 West 62nd Street, Indianapolis, Indiana 46206

Bureau of Publications, Teachers College Press, Columbia University, 525 West 120th Street, New York, New York 10027

Bureau of Educational Research and Service, Extension Division, State University of Iowa, Iowa City, Iowa 52240

California Test Bureau, Del Monte Research Park, Monterey, California 93940

Committee on Diagnostic Reading Tests, Mountain Home, North Carolina 28758

Consulting Psychologists Press, 577 College Avenue, Palo Alto, California 94306

Educational Test Bureau (see American Guidance Service)

Educational Testing Service, Princeton, New Jersey 08540

Follett Educational Corporation, 1010 West Washington Boulevard, Chicago, Illinois 60607

Ginn and Company, Waltham, Massachusetts 02154

Guidance Testing Associates, 6516 Shirley Avenue, Austin, Texas 78752

Harcourt, Brace and World, Incorporated, 757 Third Avenue, New York, New York 10017

Houghton, Mifflin Company, 2 Park Street, Boston, Massachusetts 02107

Language Research Associates, 950 East 59th Street, Chicago, Illinois 60630

Lyons and Carnahan, Incorporated, 307 East 25th Street, Chicago, Illinois 60616

The Mills Center, Incorporated, 1512 E. Broward Boulevard, Fort Lauderdale, Florida 33301

The Psychological Corporation, 304 East 45th Street, New York, New York 10017

Scholastic Testing Service, Incorporated, 480 Meyer Road, Bensenville, Illinois 60611

Science Research Associates, Incorporated, 259 East Erie Street, Chicago, Illinois 60611

Western Psychological Services, 12035 Wilshire Boulevard, Los Angeles, California 90025

Winter Haven Lions Research Foundation, Incorporated Box 112, Winter Haven, Florida 33880

Index

H

I

P

R

S

T

U

V

W